GULLIVER'S TRAVELS

Jonathan Swift

SPARK PUBLISHING

SPARKNOTES is a registered trademark of SparkNotes LLC

Spark Publishing
A Division of Barnes & Noble
120 Fifth Avenue
New York, NY 10011
www.sparknotes.com

ISBN-13: 978-1-4114-0735-0
ISBN-10: 1-4114-0735-0

Please submit changes or report errors to www.sparknotes.com/errors.

Printed in the United States.

10 9 8 7 6 5 4 3 2

CONTENTS

CONTEXT

JONATHAN SWIFT, son of the English lawyer Jonathan Swift the elder, was born in Dublin, Ireland, on November 30, 1667. He grew up there in the care of his uncle before attending Trinity College at the age of fourteen, where he stayed for seven years, graduating in 1688. In that year, he became the secretary of Sir William Temple, an English politician and member of the Whig party. In 1694, he took religious orders in the Church of Ireland and then spent a year as a country parson. He then spent further time in the service of Temple before returning to Ireland to become the chaplain of the earl of Berkeley. Meanwhile, he had begun to write satires on the political and religious corruption surrounding him, working on *A Tale of a Tub,* which supports the position of the Anglican Church against its critics on the left and the right, and *The Battle of the Books,* which argues for the supremacy of the classics against modern thought and literature. He also wrote a number of political pamphlets in favor of the Whig party. In 1709 he went to London to campaign for the Irish church but was unsuccessful. After some conflicts with the Whig party, mostly because of Swift's strong allegiance to the church, he became a member of the more conservative Tory party in 1710.

Unfortunately for Swift, the Tory government fell out of power in 1714 and Swift, despite his fame for his writings, fell out of favor. Swift, who had been hoping to be assigned a position in the Church of England, instead returned to Dublin, where he became the dean of St. Patrick's. During his brief time in England, Swift had become friends with writers such as Alexander Pope, and during a meeting of their literary club, the Martinus Scriblerus Club, they decided to write satires of modern learning. The third voyage of *Gulliver's Travels* is assembled from the work Swift did during this time. However, the final work was not completed until 1726, and the narrative of the third voyage was actually the last one completed. After his return to Ireland, Swift became a staunch supporter of the Irish against English attempts to weaken their economy and political power, writing pamphlets such as the satirical *A Modest Proposal,* in which he suggests that the Irish problems of famine and overpopulation could be easily solved by having the babies of poor Irish subjects sold as delicacies to feed the rich.

2 ✹ JONATHAN SWIFT

Gulliver's Travels was a controversial work when it was first published in 1726. In fact, it was not until almost ten years after its first printing that the book appeared with the entire text that Swift had originally intended it to have. Ever since, editors have excised many of the passages, particularly the more caustic ones dealing with bodily functions. Even without those passages, however, *Gulliver's Travels* serves as a biting satire, and Swift ensures that it is both humorous and critical, constantly attacking British and European society through its descriptions of imaginary countries.

Late in life, Swift seemed to many observers to become even more caustic and bitter than he had been. Three years before his death, he was declared unable to care for himself, and guardians were appointed. Based on these facts and on a comparison between Swift's fate and that of his character Gulliver, some people have concluded that he gradually became insane and that his insanity was a natural outgrowth of his indignation and outrage against humankind. However, the truth seems to be that Swift was suddenly incapacitated by a paralytic stroke late in life, and that prior to this incident his mental capacities were unimpaired.

Gulliver's Travels is about a specific set of political conflicts, but if it were nothing more than that it would long ago have been forgotten. The staying power of the work comes from its depiction of the human condition and its often despairing, but occasionally hopeful, sketch of the possibilities for humanity to rein in its baser instincts.

Plot Overview

ULLIVER'S TRAVELS recounts the story of Lemuel Gulliver, a practical-minded Englishman trained as a surgeon who takes to the seas when his business fails. In a deadpan first-person narrative that rarely shows any signs of self-reflection or deep emotional response, Gulliver narrates the adventures that befall him on these travels.

Gulliver's adventure in Lilliput begins when he wakes after his shipwreck to find himself bound by innumerable tiny threads and addressed by tiny captors who are in awe of him but fiercely protective of their kingdom. They are not afraid to use violence against Gulliver, though their arrows are little more than pinpricks. But overall, they are hospitable, risking famine in their land by feeding Gulliver, who consumes more food than a thousand Lilliputians combined could. Gulliver is taken into the capital city by a vast wagon the Lilliputians have specially built. He is presented to the emperor, who is entertained by Gulliver, just as Gulliver is flattered by the attention of royalty. Eventually Gulliver becomes a national resource, used by the army in its war against the people of Blefuscu, whom the Lilliputians hate for doctrinal differences concerning the proper way to crack eggs. But things change when Gulliver is convicted of treason for putting out a fire in the royal palace with his urine and is condemned to be shot in the eyes and starved to death. Gulliver escapes to Blefuscu, where he is able to repair a boat he finds and set sail for England.

After staying in England with his wife and family for two months, Gulliver undertakes his next sea voyage, which takes him to a land of giants called Brobdingnag. Here, a field worker discovers him. The farmer initially treats him as little more than an animal, keeping him for amusement. The farmer eventually sells Gulliver to the queen, who makes him a courtly diversion and is entertained by his musical talents. Social life is easy for Gulliver after his discovery by the court, but not particularly enjoyable. Gulliver is often repulsed by the physicality of the Brobdingnagians, whose ordinary flaws are many times magnified by their huge size. Thus, when a couple of courtly ladies let him play on their naked bodies, he is not attracted to them but rather disgusted by their enormous skin pores and the sound of their torrential urination. He is generally startled by the ignorance of the people here—even the king knows nothing about politics. More unsettling findings in Brobdingnag come in the form of various animals of the realm that endanger his life. Even Brobdingnagian insects leave slimy trails on his food that make eating difficult. On a trip to the frontier, accompanying the royal couple, Gulliver leaves Brobdingnag when his cage is plucked up by an eagle and dropped into the sea.

Next, Gulliver sets sail again and, after an attack by pirates, ends up in Laputa, where a floating island inhabited by theoreticians and academics oppresses the land below, called Balnibarbi. The scientific research undertaken in Laputa and in Balnibarbi seems totally inane and impractical, and its residents too appear wholly out of touch with reality. Taking a short side trip to Glubbdubdrib, Gulliver is able to witness the conjuring up of figures from history, such as Julius Caesar and other military leaders, whom he finds much less impressive than in books. After visiting the Luggnaggians and the Struldbrugs, the latter of which are senile immortals who prove that age does not bring wisdom, he is able to sail to Japan and from there back to England.

Finally, on his fourth journey, Gulliver sets out as captain of a ship, but after the mutiny of his crew and a long confinement in his cabin, he arrives in an unknown land. This land is populated by Houyhnhnms, rational-thinking horses who rule, and by Yahoos, brutish humanlike creatures who serve the Houyhnhnms. Gulliver sets about learning their language, and when he can speak he narrates his voyages to them and explains the constitution of England. He is treated with great courtesy and kindness by the horses and is enlightened by his many conversations with them and by his exposure to their noble culture. He wants to stay with the Houyhnhnms, but his bared body reveals to the horses that he is very much like a Yahoo, and he is banished. Gulliver is grief-stricken but agrees to leave. He fashions a canoe and makes his way to a nearby island, where he is picked up by a Portuguese ship captain who treats him well, though Gulliver cannot help now seeing the captain—and all humans—as shamefully Yahoolike. Gulliver then concludes his narrative with a claim that the lands he has visited belong by rights to England, as her colonies, even though he questions the whole idea of colonialism.

CHARACTER LIST

Gulliver   The narrator and protagonist of the story. Although Lemuel Gulliver's vivid and detailed style of narration makes it clear that he is intelligent and well educated, his perceptions are naïve and gullible. He has virtually no emotional life, or at least no awareness of it, and his comments are strictly factual. Indeed, sometimes his obsession with the facts of navigation, for example, becomes unbearable for us, as his fictional editor, Richard Sympson, makes clear when he explains having had to cut out nearly half of Gulliver's verbiage. Gulliver never thinks that the absurdities he encounters are funny and never makes the satiric connections between the lands he visits and his own home. Gulliver's naïveté makes the satire possible, as we pick up on things that Gulliver does not notice.

The emperor   The ruler of Lilliput. Like all Lilliputians, the emperor is fewer than six inches tall. His power and majesty impress Gulliver deeply, but to us he appears both laughable and sinister. Because of his tiny size, his belief that he can control Gulliver seems silly, but his willingness to execute his subjects for minor reasons of politics or honor gives him a frightening aspect. He is proud of possessing the tallest trees and biggest palace in the kingdom, but he is also quite hospitable, spending a fortune on his captive's food. The emperor is both a satire of the autocratic ruler and a strangely serious portrait of political power.

The farmer   Gulliver's first master in Brobdingnag. The farmer speaks to Gulliver, showing that he is willing to believe that the relatively tiny Gulliver may be as rational as he himself is, and treats him with gentleness. However, the farmer puts Gulliver on display around Brobdingnag, which clearly shows that he would rather profit from his discovery than converse with him as an equal. His exploitation of Gulliver as a laborer, which nearly starves Gulliver to death, seems less cruel than simple-minded. Generally, the farmer represents the average Brobdingnagian of no great gifts or intelligence, wielding an extraordinary power over Gulliver simply by virtue of his immense size.

Glumdalclitch The farmer's nine-year-old daughter, who is forty feet tall. Glumdalclitch becomes Gulliver's friend and nursemaid, hanging him to sleep safely in her closet at night and teaching him the Brobdingnagian language by day. She is skilled at sewing and makes Gulliver several sets of new clothes, taking delight in dressing him. When the queen discovers that no one at court is suited to care for Gulliver, she invites Glumdalclitch to live at court as his sole babysitter, a function she performs with great seriousness and attentiveness. To Glumdalclitch, Gulliver is basically a living doll, symbolizing the general status Gulliver has in Brobdingnag.

The queen The queen of Brobdingnag, who is so delighted by Gulliver's beauty and charms that she agrees to buy him from the farmer for 1,000 pieces of gold. Gulliver appreciates her kindness after the hardships he suffers at the farmer's and shows his usual fawning love for royalty by kissing the tip of her little finger when presented before her. She possesses, in Gulliver's words, "infinite" wit and humor, though this description may entail a bit of Gulliver's characteristic flattery of superiors. The queen seems genuinely considerate, asking Gulliver whether he would consent to live at court instead of simply taking him in as a pet and inquiring into the reasons for his cold good-byes with the farmer. She is by no means a hero, but simply a pleasant, powerful person.

The king The king of Brobdingnag, who, in contrast to the emperor of Lilliput, seems to be a true intellectual, well versed in political science among other disciplines. While his wife has an intimate, friendly relationship with the diminutive visitor, the king's relation to Gulliver is limited to serious discussions about the history and institutions of Gulliver's native land. He is thus a figure of rational thought who somewhat prefigures the Houyhnhnms in Book IV.

Lord Munodi A lord of Lagado, capital of the underdeveloped land beneath Laputa, who hosts Gulliver and gives him a tour of the country on Gulliver's third voyage. Munodi is a rare example of practical-minded intelligence both in Lagado, where the applied sciences are wildly impractical, and in Laputa, where no one even considers practicality a virtue. He fell from grace with the ruling elite by counseling a commonsense approach to agriculture and land management in Lagado, an approach that was rejected even though it proved successful when applied to his own flourishing estate. Lord Munodi serves as a reality check for Gulliver on his third voyage, an objective-minded contrast to the theoretical delusions of the other inhabitants of Laputa and Lagado.

Yahoos Unkempt humanlike beasts who live in servitude to the Houyhnhnms. Yahoos seem to belong to various ethnic groups, since there are blond Yahoos as well as dark-haired and redheaded ones. The men are characterized by their hairy bodies, and the women by their low-hanging breasts. They are naked, filthy, and extremely primitive in their eating habits. Yahoos are not capable of government, and thus they are kept as servants to the Houyhnhnms, pulling their carriages and performing manual tasks. They repel Gulliver with their lascivious sexual appetites, especially when an eleven-year-old Yahoo girl attempts to rape Gulliver as he is bathing naked. Yet despite Gulliver's revulsion for these disgusting creatures, he ends his writings referring to himself as a Yahoo, just as the Houyhnhnms do as they regretfully evict him from their realm. Thus, "Yahoo" becomes another term for human, at least in the semideranged and self-loathing mind of Gulliver at the end of his fourth journey.

Houyhnhnms Rational horses who maintain a simple, peaceful society governed by reason and truthfulness—they do not even have a word for "lie" in their language. Houyhnhnms are like ordinary horses, except that they are highly intelligent and deeply wise. They live in a sort of socialist republic, with the needs of the community put before individual desires. They are the masters of the Yahoos, the savage humanlike creatures in Houyhnhnmland. In all, the Houyhnhnms have the greatest impact on Gulliver throughout all his four voyages. He is grieved to leave them, not relieved as he is in leaving the other three lands, and back in England he relates better with his horses than with his human family. The Houyhnhnms thus are a measure of the extent to which Gulliver has become a misanthrope, or "human-hater"; he is certainly, at the end, a horse lover.

Gulliver's Houyhnhnm master The Houyhnhnm who first discovers Gulliver and takes him into his own home. Wary of Gulliver's Yahoolike appearance at first, the master is hesitant to make contact with him, but Gulliver's ability to mimic the Houyhnhnm's own words persuades the master to protect Gulliver. The master's domestic cleanliness, propriety, and tranquil reasonableness of speech have an extraordinary impact on Gulliver. It is through this horse that Gulliver is led to reevaluate the differences between humans and beasts and to question humanity's claims to rationality.

Don Pedro de Mendez The Portuguese captain who takes Gulliver back to Europe after he is forced to leave the land of the Houyhnhnms. Don Pedro is naturally benevolent and generous, offering the half-crazed Gulliver his own best suit of clothes to replace the tatters he is wearing. But Gulliver meets his generosity with repulsion, as he cannot bear the company of Yahoos. By the end of the voyage, Don Pedro has won over Gulliver to the extent that he is able to have a conversation with him, but the captain's overall Yahoolike nature in Gulliver's eyes alienates him from Gulliver to the very end.

Brobdingnagians Giants whom Gulliver meets on his second voyage. Brobdingnagians are basically a reasonable and kindly people governed by a sense of justice. Even the farmer who abuses Gulliver at the beginning is gentle with him, and politely takes the trouble to say good-bye to him upon leaving him. The farmer's daughter, Glumdalclitch, gives Gulliver perhaps the most kind-hearted treatment he receives on any of his voyages. The Brobdingnagians do not exploit him for personal or political reasons, as the Lilliputians do, and his life there is one of satisfaction and quietude. But the Brob-dingnagians do treat Gulliver as a plaything. When he tries to speak seriously with the king of Brobding-nag about England, the king dismisses the English as odious vermin, showing that deep discussion is not possible for Gulliver here.

Lilliputians and Blefuscudians Two races of miniature people whom Gulliver meets on his first voyage. Lilliputians and Blefuscudians are prone to conspiracies and jealousies, and while they treat Gulliver well enough materially, they are quick to take advantage of him in political intrigues of various sorts. The two races have been in a longstanding war with each over the interpretation of a reference in their common holy scripture to the proper way to eat eggs. Gulliver helps the Lilliputians defeat the Blefuscudian navy, but he eventually leaves Lilliput and receives a warm welcome in the court of Blefuscu, by which Swift satirizes the arbitrariness of international relations.

Laputans Absentminded intellectuals who live on the floating island of Laputa, encountered by Gulliver on his third voyage. The Laputans are parodies of theoreticians, who have scant regard for any practical results of their own research. They are so inwardly absorbed in their own thoughts that they must be shaken out of their meditations by special servants called flap-pers, who shake rattles in their ears. During Gulliver's stay among them, they do not mistreat him, but are generally unpleasant and dismiss him as intellectually deficient. They do not care about down-to-earth things like the dilapidation of their own houses, but worry intensely about abstract matters like the trajectories of comets and the course of the sun. They are dependent in their own material needs on the land below them, called Lagado, above which they hover by virtue of a magnetic field, and from which they periodically raise up food supplies. In the larger context of Gulliver's journeys, the Laputans are a parody of the excesses of theoretical pursuits and the uselessness of purely abstract knowledge.

Mary Burton Gulliver Gulliver's wife, whose perfunctory mention in the first paragraphs of *Gulliver's Travels* demonstrates how unsentimental and unemotional Gulliver is. He makes no reference to any affection for his wife, either here or later in his travels when he is far away from her, and his detachment is so cool as to raise questions about his ability to form human attachments. When he returns to England, she is merely one part of his former existence, and he records no emotion even as she hugs him wildly. The most important facts about her in Gulliver's mind are her social origin and the income she generates.

Richard Sympson Gulliver's cousin, self-proclaimed intimate friend, and the editor and publisher of *Gulliver's Travels*. It was in Richard Sympson's name that Jonathan Swift arranged for the publication of his narrative, thus somewhat mixing the fictional and actual worlds. Sympson is the fictional author of the prefatory note to *Gulliver's Travels,* entitled "The Publisher to the Readers." This note justifies Sympson's elimination of nearly half of the original manuscript material on the grounds that it was irrelevant, a statement that Swift includes so as to allow us to doubt Gulliver's overall wisdom and ability to distinguish between important facts and trivial details.

James Bates An eminent London surgeon under whom Gulliver serves as an apprentice after graduating from Cambridge. Bates helps get Gulliver his first job as a ship's surgeon and then offers to set up a practice with him.

After Bates's death, Gulliver has trouble maintaining the business, a failure that casts doubt on his competence, though he himself has other explanations for the business's failure. Bates is hardly mentioned in the travels, though he is surely at least as responsible for Gulliver's welfare as some of the more exotic figures Gulliver meets. Nevertheless, Gulliver fleshes out figures such as the queen of Brobdingnag much more thoroughly in his narrative, underscoring the sharp contrast between his reticence regarding England and his long-windedness about foreigners.

Abraham Pannell The commander of the ship on which Gulliver first sails, the *Swallow.* Traveling to the Levant, or the eastern Mediterranean, and beyond, Gulliver spends three and a half years on Pannell's ship. Virtually nothing is mentioned about Pannell, which heightens our sense that Gulliver's fascination with exotic types is not matched by any interest in his fellow countrymen.

William Prichard The master of the *Antelope,* the ship on which Gulliver embarks for the South Seas at the outset of his first journey, in 1699. When the *Antelope* sinks, Gulliver is washed ashore on Lilliput. No details are given about the personality of Prichard, and he is not important in Gulliver's life or in the unfolding of the novel's plot. That Gulliver takes pains to name him accurately reinforces our impression that he is obsessive about facts but not always reliable in assessing overall significance.

Flimnap The Lord High Treasurer of Lilliput, who conceives a jealous hatred for Gulliver when he starts believing that his wife is having an affair with him. Flimnap is clearly paranoid, since the possibility of a love affair between Gulliver and a Lilliputian is wildly unlikely. Flimnap is a portrait of the weaknesses of character to which any human is prone but that become especially dangerous in those who wield great power.

Reldresal   The Principal Secretary of Private Affairs in Lilliput, who explains to Gulliver the history of the political tensions between the two principal parties in the realm, the High-Heels and the Low-Heels. Reldresal is more a source of much-needed information for Gulliver than a well-developed personality, but he does display personal courage and trust in allowing Gulliver to hold him in his palm while he talks politics. Within the convoluted context of Lilliput's factions and conspiracies, such friendliness reminds us that fond personal relations may still exist even in this overheated political climate.

Skyresh Bolgolam   The High Admiral of Lilliput, who is the only member of the administration to oppose Gulliver's liberation. Gulliver imagines that Skyresh's enmity is simply personal, though there is no apparent reason for such hostility. Arguably, Skyresh's hostility may be merely a tool to divert Gulliver from the larger system of Lilliputian exploitation to which he is subjected.

Tramecksan   Also known as the High-Heels, a Lilliputian political group reminiscent of the British Tories. Tramecksan policies are said to be more agreeable to the ancient constitution of Lilliput, and while the High-Heels appear greater in number than the Low-Heels, their power is lesser. Unlike the king, the crown prince is believed to sympathize with the Tramecksan, wearing one low heel and one high heel, causing him to limp slightly.

Slamecksan   The Low-Heels, a Lilliputian political group reminiscent of the British Whigs. The king has ordained that all governmental administrators must be selected from this party, much to the resentment of the High-Heels of the realm. Thus, while there are fewer Slamecksan than Tramecksan in Lilliput, their political power is greater. The king's own sympathies with the Slamecksan are evident in the slightly lower heels he wears at court.

ANALYSIS OF MAJOR CHARACTERS

LEMUEL GULLIVER

Although Gulliver is a bold adventurer who visits a multitude of strange lands, it is difficult to regard him as truly heroic. Even well before his slide into misanthropy at the end of the book, he simply does not show the stuff of which grand heroes are made. He is not cowardly—on the contrary, he undergoes the unnerving experiences of nearly being devoured by a giant rat, taken captive by pirates, shipwrecked on faraway shores, sexually assaulted by an eleven-year-old girl, and shot in the face with poison arrows. Additionally, the isolation from humanity that he endures for sixteen years must be hard to bear, though Gulliver rarely talks about such matters. Yet despite the courage Gulliver shows throughout his voyages, his character lacks basic greatness. This impression could be due to the fact that he rarely shows his feelings, reveals his soul, or experiences great passions of any sort. But other literary adventurers, like Odysseus in Homer's *Odyssey,* seem heroic without being particularly open about their emotions.

What seems most lacking in Gulliver is not courage or feelings, but drive. One modern critic has described Gulliver as possessing the smallest will in all of Western literature: he is simply devoid of a sense of mission, a goal that would make his wandering into a quest. Odysseus's goal is to get home again, Aeneas's goal in Virgil's *Aeneid* is to found Rome, but Gulliver's goal on his sea voyage is uncertain. He says that he needs to make some money after the failure of his business, but he rarely mentions finances throughout the work and indeed almost never even mentions home. He has no awareness of any greatness in what he is doing or what he is working toward. In short, he has no aspirations. When he leaves home on his travels for the first time, he gives no impression that he regards himself as undertaking a great endeavor or embarking on a thrilling new challenge.

We may also note Gulliver's lack of ingenuity and savvy. Other great travelers, such as Odysseus, get themselves out of dangerous situations by exercising their wit and ability to trick others. Gulliver seems too dull for any battles of wit and too unimaginative to think up tricks, and thus he ends up being passive in most of the situations in which he finds himself. He is held captive several times throughout his voyages, but he is never once released through his own stratagems, relying instead on chance factors for his liberation. Once presented with a way out, he works hard to escape, as when he repairs the boat he finds that delivers him from Blefuscu, but he is never actively ingenious in attaining freedom. This example summarizes quite well Gulliver's intelligence, which is factual and practical rather than imaginative or introspective.

Gulliver is gullible, as his name suggests. For example, he misses the obvious ways in which the Lilliputians exploit him. While he is quite adept at navigational calculations and the humdrum details of seafaring, he is far less able to reflect on himself or his nation in any profoundly critical way. Traveling to such different countries and returning to England in between each voyage, he seems poised to make some great anthropological speculations about cultural differences around the world, about how societies are similar despite their variations or different despite their similarities. But, frustratingly, Gulliver gives us nothing of the sort. He provides us only with literal facts and narrative events, never with any generalizing or philosophizing. He is a self-hating, self-proclaimed Yahoo at the end, announcing his misanthropy quite loudly, but even this attitude is difficult to accept as the moral of the story. Gulliver is not a figure with whom we identify but, rather, part of the array of personalities and behaviors about which we must make judgments.

THE QUEEN OF BROBDINGNAG

The Brobdingnagian queen is hardly a well-developed character in this novel, but she is important in one sense: she is one of the very few females in *Gulliver's Travels* who is given much notice. Gulliver's own wife is scarcely even mentioned, even at what one would expect to be the touching moment of homecoming at the end of the fourth voyage. Gulliver seems little more than indifferent to his wife. The farmer's daughter in Brobdingnag wins some of Gulliver's attention but chiefly because she cares for him so tenderly. Gulliver is courteous to the empress of Lilliput but presumably mainly because she is royalty. The queen of Brobdingnag, however, arouses some deeper feelings in Gulliver that go beyond her royal status. He compliments her effusively, as he does no other female personage in the work, calling her infinitely witty and humorous. He describes in proud detail the manner in which he is permitted to kiss the tip of her little finger. For her part, the queen seems earnest in her concern about Gulliver's welfare. When her court dwarf insults him, she gives the dwarf away to another household as punishment. The interaction between Gulliver and the queen hints that Gulliver is indeed capable of emotional connections.

Lord Munodi

Lord Munodi is a minor character, but he plays the important role of showing the possibility of individual dissent within a brainwashed community. While the inhabitants of Lagado pursue their attempts to extract sunbeams from cucumbers and to eliminate all verbs and adjectives from their language, Munodi is a rare example of practical intelligence. Having tried unsuccessfully to convince his fellows of their misguided public policies, he has given up and is content to practice what he preaches on his own estates. In his kindness to strangers, Munodi is also a counterexample to the contemptuous treatment that the other Laputians and Lagadans show Gulliver. He takes his guest on a tour of the kingdom, explains the advantages of his own estates without boasting, and is, in general, a figure of great common sense and humanity amid theoretical delusions and impractical fantasizing. As a figure isolated from his community, Munodi is similar to Gulliver, though Gulliver is unaware of his alienation while Munodi suffers acutely from his. Indeed, in Munodi we glimpse what Gulliver could be if he were wiser: a figure able to think critically about life and society.

Don Pedro de Mendez

Don Pedro is a minor character in terms of plot, but he plays an important symbolic role at the end of the novel. He treats the half-deranged Gulliver with great patience, even tenderness, when he allows him to travel on his ship as far as Lisbon, offering to give him his own finest suit of clothes to replace the seaman's tatters, and giving him twenty pounds for his journey home to England. Don Pedro never judges Gulliver, despite Gulliver's abominably antisocial behavior on the trip back. Ironically, though Don Pedro shows the same kind of generosity and understanding that

Gulliver's Houyhnhnm master earlier shows him, Gulliver still considers Don Pedro a repulsive Yahoo. Were Gulliver able to escape his own delusions, he might be able to see the Houyhnhnm-like reasonableness and kindness in Don Pedro's behavior. Don Pedro is thus the touchstone through which we see that Gulliver is no longer a reliable and objective commentator on the reality he sees but, rather, a skewed observer of a reality colored by private delusions.

MARY BURTON GULLIVER

Gulliver's wife is mentioned only briefly at the beginning of the novel and appears only for an instant at the conclusion. Gulliver never thinks about Mary on his travels and never feels guilty about his lack of attention to her. A dozen far more trivial characters get much greater attention than she receives. She is, in this respect, the opposite of Odysseus's wife Penelope in the *Odyssey*, who is never far from her husband's thoughts and is the final destination of his journey. Mary's neglected presence in Gulliver's narrative gives her a certain claim to importance. It suggests that despite Gulliver's curiosity about new lands and exotic races, he is virtually indifferent to those people closest to him. His lack of interest in his wife bespeaks his underdeveloped inner life. Gulliver is a man of skill and knowledge in certain practical matters, but he is disadvantaged in self-reflection, personal interactions, and perhaps overall wisdom.

THEMES, MOTIFS & SYMBOLS

THEMES

Themes are the fundamental and often universal ideas explored in a literary work.

MIGHT VERSUS RIGHT

Gulliver's Travels implicitly poses the question of whether physical power or moral righteousness should be the governing factor in social life. Gulliver experiences the advantages of physical might both as one who has it, as a giant in Lilliput where he can defeat the Blefuscudian navy by virtue of his immense size, and as one who does not have it, as a miniature visitor to Brobdingnag where he is harassed by the hugeness of everything from insects to household pets. His first encounter with another society is one of entrapment, when he is physically tied down by the Lilliputians; later, in Brobdingnag, he is enslaved by a farmer. He also observes physical force used against others, as with the Houyhnhnms' chaining up of the Yahoos.

But alongside the use of physical force, there are also many claims to power based on moral correctness. The whole point of the egg controversy that has set Lilliput against Blefuscu is not merely a cultural difference but, instead, a religious and moral issue related to the proper interpretation of a passage in their holy book. This difference of opinion seems to justify, in their eyes at least, the warfare it has sparked. Similarly, the use of physical force against the Yahoos is justified for the Houyhnhnms by their sense of moral superiority: they are cleaner, better behaved, and more rational. But overall, the novel tends to show that claims to rule on the basis of moral righteousness are often just as arbitrary as, and sometimes simply disguises for, simple physical subjugation. The Laputans keep the lower land of Balnibarbi in check through force because they believe themselves to be more rational, even though we might see them as absurd and unpleasant. Similarly, the ruling elite of Balnibarbi believes itself to be in the right in driving Lord Munodi from power, although we perceive that Munodi is the rational party. Claims to

17

moral superiority are, in the end, as hard to justify as the random use of physical force to dominate others.

THE INDIVIDUAL VERSUS SOCIETY

Like many narratives about voyages to nonexistent lands, *Gulliver's Travels* explores the idea of utopia—an imaginary model of the ideal community. The idea of a utopia is an ancient one, going back at least as far as the description in Plato's *Republic* of a city-state governed by the wise and expressed most famously in English by Thomas More's *Utopia*. Swift nods to both works in his own narrative, though his attitude toward utopia is much more skeptical, and one of the main aspects he points out about famous historical utopias is the tendency to privilege the collective group over the individual. The children of Plato's *Republic* are raised communally, with no knowledge of their biological parents, in the understanding that this system enhances social fairness. Swift has the Lilliputians similarly raise their offspring collectively, but its results are not exactly utopian, since Lilliput is torn by conspiracies, jealousies, and backstabbing.

The Houyhnhnms also practice strict family planning, dictating that the parents of two females should exchange a child with a family of two males, so that the male-to-female ratio is perfectly maintained. Indeed, they come closer to the utopian ideal than the Lilliputians in their wisdom and rational simplicity. But there is something unsettling about the Houyhnhnms' indistinct personalities and about how they are the only social group that Gulliver encounters who do not have proper names. Despite minor physical differences, they are all so good and rational that they are more or less interchangeable, without individual identities. In their absolute fusion with their society and lack of individuality, they are in a sense the exact opposite of Gulliver, who has hardly any sense of belonging to his native society and exists only as an individual eternally wandering the seas. Gulliver's intense grief when forced to leave the Houyhnhnms may have something to do with his longing for union with a community in which he can lose his human identity. In any case, such a union is impossible for him, since he is not a horse, and all the other societies he visits make him feel alienated as well.

Gulliver's Travels could in fact be described as one of the first novels of modern alienation, focusing on an individual's repeated failures to integrate into societies to which he does not belong. England itself is not much of a homeland for Gulliver, and, with his surgeon's business unprofitable and his father's estate insufficient to support him, he may be right to feel alienated from it. He never speaks fondly or nostalgically about England, and every time he returns home, he is quick to leave again. Gulliver never complains explicitly about feeling lonely, but the embittered and antisocial misanthrope we see at the end of the novel is clearly a profoundly isolated individual. Thus, if Swift's satire mocks the excesses of communal life, it may also mock the excesses of individualism in its portrait of a miserable and lonely Gulliver talking to his horses at home in England.

THE LIMITS OF HUMAN UNDERSTANDING

The idea that humans are not meant to know everything and that all understanding has a natural limit is important in *Gulliver's Travels*. Swift singles out theoretical knowledge in particular for attack: his portrait of the disagreeable and self-centered Laputans, who show blatant contempt for those who are not sunk in private theorizing, is a clear satire against those who pride themselves on knowledge above all else. Practical knowledge is also satirized when it does not produce results, as in the academy of Balnibarbi, where the experiments for extracting sunbeams from cucumbers amount to nothing. Swift insists that there is a realm of understanding into which humans are simply not supposed to venture. Thus his depictions of rational societies, like Brobdingnag and Houyhnhnmland, emphasize not these people's knowledge or understanding of abstract ideas but their ability to live their lives in a wise and steady way.

The Brobdingnagian king knows shockingly little about the abstractions of political science, yet his country seems prosperous and well governed. Similarly, the Houyhnhnms know little about arcane subjects like astronomy, though they know how long a month is by observing the moon, since that knowledge has a practical effect on their well-being. Aspiring to higher fields of knowledge would be meaningless to them and would interfere with their happiness. In such contexts, it appears that living a happy and well-ordered life seems to be the very thing for which Swift thinks knowledge is useful.

Swift also emphasizes the importance of self-understanding. Gulliver is initially remarkably lacking in self-reflection and self-awareness. He makes no mention of his emotions, passions, dreams, or aspirations, and he shows no interest in describing his own psychology to us. Accordingly, he may strike us as frustratingly hollow

THEMES

or empty, though it is likely that his personal emptiness is part of the overall meaning of the novel. By the end, he has come close to a kind of twisted self-knowledge in his deranged belief that he is a Yahoo. His revulsion with the human condition, shown in his shabby treatment of the generous Don Pedro, extends to himself as well, so that he ends the novel in a thinly disguised state of self-hatred. Swift may thus be saying that self-knowledge has its necessary limits just as theoretical knowledge does, and that if we look too closely at ourselves we might not be able to carry on living happily.

MOTIFS

Motifs are recurring structures, contrasts, and literary devices that can help to develop and inform the text's major themes.

EXCREMENT

While it may seem a trivial or laughable motif, the recurrent mention of excrement in Gulliver's Travels actually has a serious philosophical significance in the narrative. It symbolizes everything that is crass and ignoble about the human body and about human existence in general, and it obstructs any attempt to view humans as wholly spiritual or mentally transcendent creatures. Since the Enlightenment culture of eighteenth-century England tended to view humans optimistically as noble souls rather than vulgar bodies, Swift's emphasis on the common filth of life is a slap in the face of the philosophers of his day. Thus, when Gulliver urinates to put out a fire in Lilliput, or when Brobdingnagian flies defecate on his meals, or when the scientist in Lagado works to transform excrement back into food, we are reminded how very little human reason has to do with everyday existence. Swift suggests that the human condition in general is dirtier and lowlier than we might like to believe it is.

FOREIGN LANGUAGES

Gulliver appears to be a gifted linguist, knowing at least the basics of several European languages and even a fair amount of ancient Greek. This knowledge serves him well, as he is able to disguise himself as a Dutchman in order to facilitate his entry into Japan, which at the time only admitted the Dutch. But even more important, his linguistic gifts allow him to learn the languages of the exotic lands he visits with a dazzling speed and, thus, gain access to their culture quickly. He learns the languages of the Lilliputians, the Brobdingnagians, and even the neighing tongue of the Houyhnhnms. He is meticulous in recording the details of language in his narrative, often giving the original as well as the translation. One would expect that such detail would indicate a cross-cultural sensitivity, a kind of anthropologist's awareness of how things vary from culture to culture. Yet surprisingly, Gulliver's mastery of foreign languages generally does not correspond to any real interest in cultural differences. He compares any of the governments he visits to that of his native England, and he rarely even speculates on how or why cultures are different at all. Thus, his facility for translation does not indicate a culturally comparative mind, and we are perhaps meant to yearn for a narrator who is a bit less able to remember the Brobdingnagian word for "lark" and better able to offer a more illuminating kind of cultural analysis.

CLOTHING

Critics have noted the extraordinary attention that Gulliver pays to clothes throughout his journeys. Every time he gets a rip in his shirt or is forced to adopt some native garment to replace one of his own, he recounts the clothing details with great precision. We are told how his pants are falling apart in Lilliput, so that as the army marches between his legs they get quite an eyeful. We are informed about the mouse skin he wears in Brobdingnag, and how the finest silks of the land are as thick as blankets on him. In one sense, these descriptions are obviously an easy narrative device with which Swift can chart his protagonist's progression from one culture to another: the more ragged his clothes become and the stranger his new wardrobe, the farther he is from the comforts and conventions of England. His journey to new lands is also thus a journey into new clothes. When he is picked up by Don Pedro after his fourth voyage and offered a new suit of clothes, Gulliver vehemently refuses, preferring his wild animal skins. We sense that Gulliver may well never fully reintegrate into European society.

But the motif of clothing carries a deeper, more psychologically complex meaning as well. Gulliver's intense interest in the state of his clothes may signal a deep-seated anxiety about his identity, or lack thereof. He does not seem to have much selfhood: one critic has called him an "abyss," a void where an individual character should be. If clothes make the man, then perhaps Gulliver's obsession with the state of his wardrobe may suggest that he desperately needs to be fashioned as a personality. Significantly, the two moments when he describes being naked in the novel are two deeply troubling or humiliating experiences: the first when he is the boy toy of the Brobdingnagian maids who let him cavort nude on their mountainous breasts, and the second when he is assaulted by an eleven-year-old Yahoo girl as he bathes. Both incidents suggest more than mere prudery. Gulliver associates nudity with extreme vulnerability, even when there is no real danger present—a pre-teen girl is hardly a threat to a grown man, at least in physical terms. The state of nudity may remind Gulliver of how nonexistent he feels without the reassuring cover of clothing.

SYMBOLS

Symbols are objects, characters, figures, and colors used to represent abstract ideas or concepts.

LILLIPUTIANS

The Lilliputians symbolize humankind's wildly excessive pride in its own puny existence. Swift fully intends the irony of representing the tiniest race visited by Gulliver as by far the most vainglorious and smug, both collectively and individually. There is surely no character more odious in all of Gulliver's travels than the noxious Skyresh. There is more backbiting and conspiracy in Lilliput than anywhere else, and more of the pettiness of small minds who imagine themselves to be grand. Gulliver is a naïve consumer of the Lilliputians' grandiose imaginings: he is flattered by the attention of their royal family and cowed by their threats of punishment, forgetting that they have no real physical power over him. Their formally worded condemnation of Gulliver on grounds of treason is a model of pompous and self-important verbiage, but it works quite effectively on the naïve Gulliver.

The Lilliputians show off not only to Gulliver but to themselves as well. There is no mention of armies proudly marching in any of the other societies Gulliver visits—only in Lilliput and neighboring Blefuscu are the six-inch inhabitants possessed of the need to show off their patriotic glories with such displays. When the Lilliputian emperor requests that Gulliver serve as a kind of makeshift Arch of Triumph for the troops to pass under, it is a pathetic reminder that their grand parade—in full view of Gulliver's nether regions—is supremely silly, a basically absurd way to boost the collective ego of the nation. Indeed, the war with Blefuscu is itself an absurdity springing from wounded vanity, since the cause is not a material concern like disputed territory but, rather, the proper interpretation

of scripture by the emperor's forebears and the hurt feelings resulting from the disagreement. All in all, the Lilliputians symbolize mis-
placed human pride, and point out Gulliver's inability to diagnose
it correctly.

BROBDINGNAGIANS
The Brobdingnagians symbolize the private, personal, and physical side of humans when examined up close and in great detail.
The philosophical era of the Enlightenment tended to overlook
the routines of everyday life and the sordid or tedious little facts
of existence, but in Brobdingnag such facts become very important
for Gulliver, sometimes matters of life and death. An eighteenth-
century philosopher could afford to ignore the fly buzzing around
his head or the skin pores on his servant girl, but in his shrunken
state Gulliver is forced to pay great attention to such things. He is
forced to take the domestic sphere seriously as well. In other lands
it is difficult for Gulliver, being such an outsider, to get glimpses of
family relations or private affairs, but in Brobdingnag he is treated
as a doll or a plaything, and thus is made privy to the urination
of housemaids and the sexual lives of women. The Brobdingnagians do not symbolize a solely negative human characteristic, as the
Laputans do. They are not merely ridiculous—some aspects of them
are disgusting, like their gigantic stench and the excrement left by
their insects, but others are noble, like the queen's goodwill toward
Gulliver and the king's commonsense views of politics. More than
anything else, the Brobdingnagians symbolize a dimension of human existence visible at close range, under close scrutiny.

LAPUTANS
The Laputans represent the folly of theoretical knowledge that has
no relation to human life and no use in the actual world. As a pro-
found cultural conservative, Swift was a critic of the newfangled
ideas springing up around him at the dawn of the eighteenth-
century Enlightenment, a period of great intellectual experimenta-
tion and theorization. He much preferred the traditional knowledge
that had been tested over centuries. Laputa symbolizes the absurdity
of knowledge that has never been tested or applied, the ludicrous
side of Enlightenment intellectualism. Even down below in Balnibarbi, where the local academy is more inclined to practical
application, knowledge is not made socially useful as Swift
demands. Indeed, theoretical knowledge there has proven positively
disastrous, resulting in the ruin of agriculture and architecture and

the impoverishment of the population. Even up above, the pursuit of theoretical understanding has not improved the lot of the Laputans. They have few material worries, dependent as they are upon the Balnibarbians below. But they are tormented by worries about the trajectories of comets and other astronomical speculations: their theories have not made them wise, but neurotic and disagreeable. The Laputans do not symbolize reason itself but rather the pursuit of a form of knowledge that is not directly related to the improvement of human life.

HOUYHNHNMS

The Houyhnhnms represent an ideal of rational existence, a life governed by sense and moderation of which philosophers since Plato have long dreamed. Indeed, there are echoes of Plato's *Republic* in the Houyhnhnms' rejection of light entertainment and vain displays of luxury, their appeal to reason rather than any holy writings as the criterion for proper action, and their communal approach to family planning. As in Plato's ideal community, the Houyhnhnms have no need to lie nor any word for lying. They do not use force but only strong exhortation. Their subjugation of the Yahoos appears more necessary than cruel and perhaps the best way to deal with an unfortunate blot on their otherwise ideal society. In these ways and others, the Houyhnhnms seem like model citizens, and Gulliver's intense grief when he is forced to leave them suggests that they have made an impact on him greater than that of any other society he has visited. His derangement on Don Pedro's ship, in which he snubs the generous man as a Yahoo-like creature, implies that he strongly identifies with the Houyhnhnms.

But we may be less ready than Gulliver to take the Houyhnhnms as ideals of human existence. They have no names in the narrative nor any need for names, since they are virtually interchangeable, with little individual identity. Their lives seem harmonious and happy, although quite lacking in vigor, challenge, and excitement. Indeed, this apparent ease may be why Swift chooses to make them horses rather than human types like every other group in the novel. He may be hinting, to those more insightful than Gulliver, that the Houyhnhnms should not be considered human ideals at all. In any case, they symbolize a standard of rational existence to be either espoused or rejected by both Gulliver and us.

ENGLAND

As the site of his father's disappointingly "small estate" and Gulliver's failing business, England seems to symbolize deficiency or insufficiency, at least in the financial sense that matters most to Gulliver. England is passed over very quickly in the first paragraph of Chapter I, as if to show that it is simply there as the starting point to be left quickly behind. Gulliver seems to have very few nationalistic or patriotic feelings about England, and he rarely mentions his homeland on his travels. In this sense, *Gulliver's Travels* is quite unlike other travel narratives like the *Odyssey*, in which Odysseus misses his homeland and laments his wanderings. England is where Gulliver's wife and family live, but they too are hardly mentioned. Yet Swift chooses to have Gulliver return home after each of his four journeys instead of having him continue on one long trip to four different places, so that England is kept constantly in the picture and given a steady, unspoken importance. By the end of the fourth journey, England is brought more explicitly into the fabric of *Gulliver's Travels* when Gulliver, in his neurotic state, starts confusing Houyhnhnmland with his homeland, referring to Englishmen as Yahoos. The distinction between native and foreign thus unravels— the Houyhnhnms and Yahoos are not just races populating a faraway land but rather types that Gulliver projects upon those around him. The possibility thus arises that all the races Gulliver encounters could be versions of the English and that his travels merely allow him to see various aspects of human nature more clearly.

Summary & Analysis

Part I, Chapter I

SUMMARY

> *My Father had a small Estate in Nottinghamshire; I*
> *was the Third of five Sons.*
> (See QUOTATIONS, *p. 60)*

The novel begins with Lemuel Gulliver recounting the story of his life, beginning with his family history. He is born to a family in Nottinghamshire, the third of five sons. Although he studies at Cambridge as a teenager, his family is too poor to keep him there, so he is sent to London to be a surgeon's apprentice. There, under a man named James Bates, he learns mathematics and navigation with the hope of traveling. When his apprenticeship ends, he studies physics at Leyden.

He then becomes a surgeon aboard a ship called the *Swallow* for three years. Afterward, he settles in London, working as a doctor, and marries a woman named Mary Burton. His business begins to fail when his patron dies, so he decides to go to sea again and travels for six years. Although he has planned to return home at the end of this time, he decides to accept one last job on a ship called the *Antelope.*

In the East Indies, the *Antelope* encounters a violent storm in which twelve crewmen die. Six of the crewmembers, including Gulliver, board a small rowboat to escape. Soon the rowboat capsizes, and Gulliver loses track of his companions. They are never seen again. Gulliver, however, swims safely to shore.

Gulliver lies down on the grass to rest, and soon he falls asleep. When he wakes up, he finds that his arms, legs, and long hair have been tied to the ground with pieces of thread. He can only look up, and the bright sun prevents him from seeing anything. He feels something move across his leg and over his chest. He looks down and sees, to his surprise, a six-inch-tall human carrying a bow and arrow. At least forty more little people climb onto his body. He is surprised and shouts loudly, frightening the little people away. They return, however, and one of the little men cries out, "*Hekinah Degul.*"

Gulliver struggles to get loose and finally succeeds in breaking the strings binding his left arm. He loosens the ropes tying his hair so he can turn to the left. In response, the little people fire a volley of arrows into his hand and violently attack his body and face. He decides that the safest thing to do is to lie still until nightfall. The noise increases as the little people build a stage next to Gulliver about a foot and a half off the ground. One of them climbs onto it and makes a speech in a language that Gulliver does not understand.

Gulliver indicates that he is hungry, and the little people bring him baskets of meat. He devours it all and then shows that he is thirsty, so they bring him two large barrels of wine. Gulliver is tempted to pick up forty or fifty of the little people and throw them against the ground, but he decides that he has made them a promise of goodwill and is grateful for their hospitality. He is also struck by their bravery, since they climb onto his body despite his great size.

An official climbs onto Gulliver's body and tells him that he is to be carried to the capital city. Gulliver wants to walk, but they tell him that that will not be permitted. Instead, they bring a frame of wood raised three inches off the ground and carried by twenty-two wheels. Nine hundred men pull this cart about half a mile to the city. Gulliver's left leg is then padlocked to a large temple, giving him only enough freedom to walk around the building in a semicircle and lie down inside the temple.

ANALYSIS

Gulliver's narrative begins much like other travel records of his time. The description of his youth and education provides background knowledge, establishes Gulliver's position in English society, and causes the novel to resemble true-life accounts of travels at sea published during Swift's lifetime. Swift imitates the style of a standard travelogue throughout the novel to heighten the satire. Here he creates a set of expectations in our minds, namely a short-lived belief in the truth of Gulliver's observations. Later in the novel, Swift uses the style of the travelogue to exaggerate the absurdity of the people and places with which Gulliver comes into contact. A fantastical style—one that made no attempt to seem truthful, accurate, or traditional—would have weakened the satire by making it irrelevant, but the factual, reportorial style of *Gulliver's Travels* does the opposite.

Gulliver is surprised to discover the Lilliputians but is not particularly shocked. This encounter is only the first of many in the novel in which we are asked to accept Gulliver's extraordinary experiences as merely unusual. Seeing the world through Gulliver's eyes, we also adopt, for a moment, Gulliver's view of the world. But at the same time, we can step back and recognize that the Lilliputians are nothing but a figment of Swift's imagination. The distance between these two stances—the gullible Gulliver and the skeptical reader—is where the narrative's multiple levels of meaning are created: on one level, we have a true-life story of adventure; on another, a purely fictional fairy tale; and on a third level, transcending the first two and closest to Swift's original intention, a satirical critique of European pretensions to rationality and goodwill.

Swift wrote *Gulliver's Travels* at a time when Europe was the world's dominant power, and when England, despite its small size, was rising in power on the basis of its formidable fleet. England's growing military and economic power brought it into contact with a wide variety of new animals, plants, places, and things, but the most significant change wrought by European expansion was the encounter with previously unknown people—like the inhabitants of the Americas—with radically different modes of existence. The miniature stature of the Lilliputians can be interpreted as a physical incarnation of exactly these kinds of cultural differences.

The choice of physical size as the way of manifesting cultural differences has a number of important consequences. The main consequence is the radical difference in power between Gulliver and the Lilliputian nation. His physical size and strength put Gulliver in a unique position within Lilliputian society and give him obligations and capabilities far beyond those of the people who keep him prisoner. Despite Gulliver's fear of the Lilliputians' arrows, there is an element of condescension in his willingness to be held prisoner by them. The power differential may represent England's position with respect to the people it was in the process of colonizing. It may also be a way for Swift to reveal the importance of might in a society supposedly guided by right. Finally, it may be a way of destabilizing humanity's position at the center of the universe by demonstrating that size, power, and significance are all relative. Although the Lilliputians are almost pitifully small in Gulliver's eyes, they are unwilling to see themselves that way; rather, they think of themselves as normal and of Gulliver as a freakish giant. That Gulliver may himself be the Lilliputian to some other nation's Englishman—a notion elaborated fully in Part II—is already implied in the first chapter.

Part I, Chapters II–III

Summary: Chapter II

Once the Lilliputians chain Gulliver to the building, he is finally allowed to stand up and view the entire countryside, which he discovers is beautiful and rustic. The tallest trees are seven feet tall, and the whole area looks to him like a theater set.

Gulliver meticulously describes his process of relieving himself, which initially involves walking inside the building to the edge of his chain. After the first time, he makes sure to relieve himself in open air, and servants carry away his excrement in wheelbarrows. He says that he describes this process in order to establish his cleanliness, which has been called into question by his critics.

The emperor visits on horseback from his tower. He orders his servants to give Gulliver food and drink. The emperor is dressed plainly and carries a sword to defend himself. He and Gulliver converse, though they cannot understand each other. Gulliver tries to speak every language he knows, but nothing works. After two hours, Gulliver is left with a group of soldiers guarding him. Some of them, disobeying orders, try to shoot arrows at him. As a punishment, the brigadier ties up six of these offenders and places them in Gulliver's hand. Gulliver puts five of them into his pocket and pretends that he is going to eat the sixth, but then cuts loose his ropes and sets him free. He does the same with the other five, which pleases the court.

After two weeks, a bed is made for Gulliver. It consists of 600 small beds sewn together. News of his arrival also spreads throughout the kingdom and curious people from the villages come to see him. Meanwhile, the government tries to decide what to do with him. Frequent councils bring up various concerns: that he will break loose, for instance, or that he will eat enough to cause a famine. Some suggest that they starve him or shoot him in the face to kill him, but others argue that doing so would leave them with a giant corpse and a large health risk.

Officers who witnessed Gulliver's lenient treatment of the six offending soldiers report to the council, and the emperor and his court decide to respond with kindness. They arrange to deliver large amounts of food to Gulliver every morning, supply him with servants to wait on him, hire tailors to make him clothing, and offer teachers to instruct him in their language.

Every morning Gulliver asks the emperor to set him free, but the emperor refuses, saying that Gulliver must be patient. The emperor also orders him to be searched to ensure that he does not have any weapons. Gulliver agrees to this search, and the Lilliputians take an inventory of his possessions. In the process, all of his weapons are taken away.

SUMMARY: CHAPTER III

Gulliver hopes to be set free, as he is getting along well with the Lilliputians and earning their trust. The emperor decides to entertain him with shows, including a performance by Rope-Dancers, who are Lilliputians seeking employment in the government. For the performance, which doubles as a sort of competitive entrance examination, the candidates dance on "ropes"—slender threads suspended two feet above the ground. When a vacancy occurs, candidates petition the emperor to entertain him with a dance, and whoever jumps the highest earns the office. The current ministers continue this practice as well, in order to show that they have not lost their skill.

As another diversion for Gulliver, the emperor lays three silken threads of different colors on a table. He then holds out a stick, and candidates are asked to leap over it or creep under it. Whoever shows the most dexterity wins one of the ribbons.

Gulliver builds a platform from sticks and his handkerchief and invites horsemen to exercise upon it. The emperor greatly enjoys watching this new entertainment, but it is cut short when a horse steps through the handkerchief, after which Gulliver decides that it is too dangerous for them to keep riding on the cloth.

Some Lilliputians discover Gulliver's hat, which washed ashore after him, and he asks them to bring it back. Soon after, the emperor asks Gulliver to pose like a colossus, or giant statue, so that his troops might march under Gulliver.

Gulliver's petitions for freedom are finally answered. Gulliver must swear to obey the articles put forth, which include stipulations that he must assist the Lilliputians in times of war, survey the land around them, help with construction, and deliver urgent messages. Gulliver agrees and his chains are removed.

ANALYSIS: PART I, CHAPTERS II–III

In these chapters, Gulliver learns more about Lilliputian culture, and the great difference in size between him and the Lilliputians is emphasized by a number of examples, many of which are explicit satires of British government. For instance, Lilliputian government officials are chosen by their skill at rope-dancing, which the Lilliputians see as relevant but which Gulliver recognizes as arbitrary and ridiculous. The would-be officials are almost literally forced to jump through hoops in order to qualify for their positions. Clearly, Swift intends for us to understand this episode as a satire of England's system of political appointments and to infer that England's system is similarly arbitrary. Gulliver, however, never suggests that *he* finds the Lilliputians ridiculous. Throughout the entire novel, Gulliver tends to be very sympathetic in his descriptions of the cultures he visits, never criticizing them or finding anything funny, no matter how ludicrous certain customs seem to us. Nor does Gulliver point out the similarities between the ridiculous practices he observes in his travels and the ridiculous customs of Europe. Instead, Swift leaves us to infer all of the satire based on the difference between how things appear to us and how they appear to Gulliver.

The difference in size between Gulliver and the Lilliputians helps to emphasize the importance of physical power, a theme that recurs throughout the novel. Over time, Gulliver begins to earn the Lilliputians' trust, but it is clearly unnecessary: for all their threats, Gulliver could crush the Lilliputians by simply walking carelessly. The humor comes from the Lilliputians' view of the situation: despite the evidence before their eyes, they never realize their own insignificance. They keep Gulliver tied up, believing that they can control him, while in truth he could destroy them effortlessly. In this way, Swift satirizes humanity's pretensions to power and significance.

In these chapters, Swift plays with language in a way that again pokes fun at humanity's belief in its own importance. When the Lilliputians draw up an inventory of Gulliver's possessions, the whole endeavor is treated as if it were a serious matter of state. The contrast between the tone of the inventory, which is given in the Lilliputians' own words, and the utter triviality of the possessions that are being inventoried, serves as a mockery of people who take themselves too seriously. Similarly, the articles that Gulliver is forced to sign in order to gain his freedom are couched in formal, self-important language. But the document is nothing but a meaningless and self-contradictory piece of paper: each article emphasizes the fact that Gulliver is so powerful that, if he so desires, he could violate all of the articles without much concern for his own safety.

PART I, CHAPTERS IV–V

SUMMARY: CHAPTER IV

After regaining his freedom, Gulliver goes to Mildendo, the capital city of the Lilliputians. The residents are told to stay indoors, and they all sit on their roofs and in their garret windows to see him. The town is 500 feet square with a wall surrounding it, and can hold 500,000 people. The emperor wants Gulliver to see the magnificence of his palace, which is at the center of the city, so Gulliver cuts down trees to make himself a stool, which he carries around with him so that he can sit down and see things from a shorter distance than a standing position allows.

About two weeks after Gulliver obtains his liberty, a government official, Reldresal, comes to see him. He tells Gulliver that two forces, one rebel group and one foreign empire, threaten the kingdom. The rebel group exists because the kingdom is divided into two factions, called Tramecksan and Slamecksan. The people in the two factions are distinguished by the heights of their heels.

Reldresal tells Gulliver that the current emperor has chosen to employ primarily the low-heeled Slamecksan in his administration. He adds that the emperor himself has lower heels than all of his officials but that his heir has one heel higher than the other, which makes him walk unevenly. At the same time, the Lilliputians fear an invasion from the Island of Blefuscu, which Reldresal calls the "Other Great Empire of the Universe." He adds that the philosophers of Lilliput do not believe Gulliver's claim that there are other countries in the world inhabited by other people of his size, preferring to think that Gulliver dropped from the moon or a star.

Reldresal describes the history of the two nations. The conflict between them, he tells Gulliver, began years ago, when the emperor's grandfather, then in command of the country, commanded all Lilliputians to break their eggs on the small end first. He made this decision after breaking an egg in the old way, large end first, and cutting his finger. The people resented the law, and six rebellions were started in protest. The monarchs of Blefuscu fueled these rebellions, and when they were over the rebels fled to that country to seek refuge. Eleven thousand people chose death rather than submit to the law. Many books were written on the controversy, but books written by the Big-Endians were banned in Lilliput. The government of Blefuscu accused the Lilliputians of disobeying their religious doctrine, the *Brundrecral*, by breaking their eggs at the small end. The Lilliputians argued that the doctrine reads, "That all true believers shall break their eggs at the convenient end," which could be interpreted as the small end.

Reldresal continues that the exiles gained support in Blefuscu to launch a war against Lilliput and were aided by rebel forces inside Lilliput. A war has been raging between the two nations ever since, and Gulliver is asked to help defend Lilliput against its enemies. Gulliver does not feel that it is appropriate to intervene, but he nonetheless offers his services to the emperor.

SUMMARY: CHAPTER V

Gulliver spies on the empire of Blefuscu and devises a plan. He asks for cables and bars of iron, out of which he makes hooks with cables attached. He then wades and swims the channel to Blefuscu and catches their ships at port. The people are so frightened that they leap out of their ships and swim to shore. Gulliver attaches a hook to each ship and ties them together. The Blefuscu soldiers fire arrows at him, but he keeps working, protecting his eyes by putting on the spectacles he keeps in his coat pocket. He tries to pull the ships away, but they are anchored too tightly, so he cuts them away with his pocketknife and pulls the ships back to Lilliput.

In Lilliput, Gulliver is greeted as a hero. The emperor asks him to go back to retrieve the other ships, intending to destroy Blefuscu's military strength and make it a province in his empire. Gulliver dissuades him from this action, saying that he does not want to encourage slavery or injustice. This position causes great disagreement in the government, with some officials turning staunchly against Gulliver and calling for his destruction.

Three weeks later, a delegation arrives from Blefuscu, and the war ends with Blefuscu's surrender. The Blefuscu delegates are privately told of Gulliver's kindness toward the Lilliputians, and they ask him to visit their kingdom. He wishes to do so, and the emperor reluctantly allows it.

As a *Nardac,* or person of high rank, Gulliver no longer has to perform all the duties laid down in his contract. He does, however, have the opportunity to help the Lilliputians when the emperor's wife's room catches fire. He forgets his coat and cannot put the flames out with his clothing, so instead he thinks of a new plan: he urinates on the palace, putting out the fire entirely. He worries afterward that since the act of public urination is a crime in Lilliput he will be prosecuted, but the emperor tells him he will be pardoned. He is told, however, that the emperor's wife can no longer tolerate living in her rescued quarters.

ANALYSIS: PART I, CHAPTERS IV–V

Despite the fact that the history of the conflict between Lilliput and Blefuscu is blatantly ridiculous, Gulliver reports it with complete seriousness. The more serious the tone, the more laughable this conflict appears. But Swift expects us to understand immediately that the entire history Gulliver relates parallels European history exactly, down to the smallest details. The High-Heels and the Low-Heels correspond to the Whigs and Tories of English politics. Lilliput and Blefuscu represent England and France. The violent conflict between Big-Endians and Little-Endians represents the Protestant Reformation and the centuries of warfare between Catholics and Protestants.

By recasting European history as a series of brutal wars over meaningless and arbitrary disagreements, Swift implies that the differences between Protestants and Catholics, between Whigs and Tories, and between France and England are as silly and meaningless as how a person chooses to crack an egg. Once we make this connection, though, we face the question of *why* Swift thinks that these conflicts are trivial and irrelevant. After all, religion, politics, and national identity would have been considered the most important issues in Swift's time, and we continue to think of these things as important today. The answer to this question is less obvious, and the text does not give us a simple explanation. The debate between the Big-Endians and Little-Endians does provide some clues, however. The egg controversy is ridiculous because there cannot be any right or wrong way to crack an egg, so it is unreasonable to legislate how people must do it. Similarly, we may conclude that there is no right or wrong way to worship God—at least, there is no way to prove that one way is right and another way is wrong. Moreover, the Big-Endians and Little-Endians both share the same religious text, but they disagree on how to interpret a passage that can clearly be interpreted two ways. Similarly, Swift is suggesting that the Christian Bible can be interpreted in more than one way, and that it is ridiculous for people to fight over how to interpret it when no one can really be certain that one interpretation is right and others are wrong.

The text contains a number of allusions to events in Swift's life and to the politics of Europe. For instance, it has been suggested that the empress represents Queen Anne of England, Gulliver's urination on her quarters represents Swift's work *A Tale of a Tub,* and the empress's disgust at Gulliver's urination is analogous to Queen Anne's criticism of Swift's work and her attempts to limit his prospects in the Church of England. Within the story, Gulliver's urination on the palace is not merely an offense to the Lilliputians' sense of decency, it is also a suggestion of their insignificance, to which they respond indignantly. Although Gulliver's urination is intended to prevent a disaster, it is also an assertion of his ability to control the Lilliputians—even by the most profane of actions. The episode illustrates again the importance of physical power, which can turn a normally insignificant and vulgar action into a lifesaving act.

Gulliver's refusal to obey the emperor's orders to destroy the fleet of Blefuscu is a sign that he feels some responsibility toward all beings. However small, the inhabitants of Blefuscu still have rights, one of which is freedom from tyranny. Granted almost godlike power by his unusual size, Gulliver finds himself in a position to change the Lilliputians' society forever.

PART I, CHAPTERS VI–VIII

SUMMARY: CHAPTER VI

Gulliver describes the general customs and practices of Lilliput in more detail, beginning by explaining that everything in Lilliput—their animals, trees, and plants—is sized in proportion to the Lilliputians. Their eyesight is also adapted to their scale: Gulliver cannot see as clearly close-up as they can, while they cannot see as far as he can.

The Lilliputians are well educated, but their writing system is odd to Gulliver, who jokes that they write not left to right like the Europeans or top to bottom like the Chinese, but from one corner of the page to the other, "like the ladies in England."

The dead are buried with their heads pointing directly downward, because the Lilliputians believe that eventually the dead will rise again and that the Earth, which they think is flat, will turn upside down. Gulliver adds that the better-educated Lilliputians no longer believe in this custom.

Gulliver describes some of the other laws of Lilliput, such as a tradition by which anyone who falsely accuses someone else of a crime against the state is put to death. Deceit is considered worse than theft, because honest people are more vulnerable to liars than to thieves, since commerce requires people to trust one another. The law provides not only for punishment but also for rewards of special titles and privileges for good behavior.

Children are raised not by individual parents but by the kingdom as a whole. They are sent to live in schools at a very young age. The schools are chosen according to the station of their parents, whom they see only twice a year. Only the laborers' children stay home, since their job is to farm. There are no beggars at all, since the poor are well looked after.

SUMMARY: CHAPTER VII

Gulliver goes on to describe the "intrigue" that precipitates his departure from Lilliput. While he prepares to make his trip to Blefuscu, a court official tells Gulliver that he has been charged with treason by enemies in the government. He shows Gulliver the document calling for his execution: Gulliver is charged with public urination, refusing to obey the emperor's orders to seize the remaining Blefuscu ships, aiding enemy ambassadors, and traveling to Blefuscu.

Gulliver is told that Reldresal has asked for his sentence to be reduced, calling not for execution but for putting his eyes out. This punishment has been agreed upon, along with a plan to starve him to death slowly. The official tells Gulliver that the operation to blind him will take place in three days. Fearing this resolution, Gulliver crosses the channel and arrives in Blefuscu.

SUMMARY: CHAPTER VIII

Three days later, he sees a boat of normal size—that is, big enough to carry him—overturned in the water. He asks the emperor of Blefuscu to help him fix it. At the same time, the emperor of Lilliput sends an envoy with the articles commanding Gulliver to give up his eyesight. The emperor of Blefuscu sends it back with the message that Gulliver will soon be leaving both their kingdoms. After about a month, the boat is ready and Gulliver sets sail. He arrives safely back in England, where he makes a good profit showing miniature farm animals that he carried away from Blefuscu in his pockets.

ANALYSIS: PART I, CHAPTERS VI–VIII

Throughout much of Part I, Swift satirizes European practices by implicitly comparing them to outrageous Lilliputian customs. In Chapter VI, however, Gulliver describes a number of unusual Lilliputian customs that he presents as reasonable and sensible. This chapter, which describes improvements that could be made in European society, is less satirical and ironic than the previous chapters. We may infer that Swift approves of many of these institutions. Clearly, there is a good case to be made for treating fraud as a more serious crime than theft and for making false testimony a capital crime. The very fabric of society depends upon trust, so dishonesty may be even more damaging than theft and violence.

In general, the customs of Lilliput that Swift presents as good are those that contribute to the good of the community or the nation as opposed to those that promote individual rights or freedoms.

Ingratitude is punishable by death, for instance, because anybody who would treat a benefactor badly must be an enemy to all mankind. Children are raised by the community rather than by their parents because parents are thinking only of their own appetites when they conceive children. Children are raised in public nurseries, but parents are financially penalized if they burden society by bringing children for whom they cannot pay into the world.

Gulliver's analysis of Lilliputian customs also serves to illuminate the arbitrary nature of such practices, as well as the fact that societies tend to assume, nonetheless, that certain customs are simply natural. The Lilliputians do not question their cultural norms because they have no reason to believe that there is any other way to conduct affairs. When alternatives are discussed, as in the case of the egg-breaking controversy, the discussion ends in violent conflict.

The articles of accusation against Gulliver, like the inventory of his possessions and the articles of his freedom in the previous chapters, are written in formal language that serves only to emphasize their absurdity. Swift makes a mockery of formal language by showing how it can be used to mask simple fears and desires, such as the Lilliputians' desire to eliminate the threat that Gulliver poses. The help that Gulliver gets from Reldresal is an illustration of a persistent motif in *Gulliver's Travels:* the good person surrounded by a corrupt society.

PART II, CHAPTERS I–II

SUMMARY: CHAPTER I

Two months after returning to England, Gulliver is restless again. He sets sail on a ship called the *Adventure,* traveling to the Cape of Good Hope and Madagascar before encountering a monsoon that draws the ship off course. The ship eventually arrives at an unknown land mass. There are no inhabitants about, and the landscape is barren and rocky. Gulliver is walking back to the boat when he sees that it has already left without him. He tries to chase after it, but then he sees that a giant is following the boat. Gulliver runs away, and when he stops, he is on a steep hill from which he can see the countryside. He is shocked to see that the grass is about twenty feet high.

He walks down what looks like a high road but turns out to be a footpath through a field of barley. He walks for a long time but cannot see anything beyond the stalks of corn, which are forty feet high. He tries to climb a set of steps into the next field, but he cannot mount them because they are too high. As he is trying to climb up the stairs, he sees another one of the island's giant inhabitants. He hides from the giant, but it calls for more people to come, and they begin to harvest the crop with scythes. Gulliver lies down and bemoans his state, thinking about how insignificant he must be to these giant creatures.

One of the servants comes close to Gulliver with both his foot and his scythe, so Gulliver screams as loudly as he can. The giant finally notices him, and picks him up between his fingers to get a closer look. Gulliver tries to speak to him in plaintive tones, bringing his hands together, and the giant seems pleased. Gulliver makes it clear that the giant's fingers are hurting him, and the giant places him in his pocket and begins to walk toward his master.

The giant's master, the farmer of these fields, takes Gulliver from his servant and observes him more closely. He asks the other servants if they have ever seen anything like Gulliver, then places him onto the ground. They sit around him in a circle. Gulliver kneels down and begins to speak as loudly as he can, taking off his hat and bowing to the farmer. He presents a purse full of gold to the farmer, which the farmer takes into his palm. He cannot figure out what it is, even after Gulliver empties the coins into his hand.

The farmer takes Gulliver back to his wife, who is frightened of him. The servant brings in dinner, and they all sit down to eat, Gulliver sitting on the table not far from the farmer's plate. They give him tiny bits of their food, and he pulls out his knife and fork to eat, which delights the giants. The farmer's son picks Gulliver up and scares him, but the farmer takes Gulliver from the boy's hands and strikes his son. Gulliver makes a sign that the boy should be forgiven, and kisses his hand. After dinner, the farmer's wife lets Gulliver nap in her own bed. When he wakes up he finds two rats attacking him, and he defends himself with his "hanger," or sword.

SUMMARY: CHAPTER II

The farmer's nine-year-old daughter, whom Gulliver calls Glumdalclitch, or "nursemaid," has a doll's cradle that becomes Gulliver's permanent bed. Glumdalclitch places the cradle inside a drawer to keep Gulliver safe from the rats. She becomes Gulliver's caretaker and guardian, sewing clothes for him and teaching him the giants' language.

The farmer begins to talk about Gulliver in town, and a friend of the farmer's comes to see him. He looks at Gulliver through his glasses, and Gulliver begins to laugh at the sight of the man's eyes through the glass. The man becomes angry and advises the farmer to take Gulliver into the market to display him. He agrees, and Gulliver is taken to town in a carriage, which he finds very uncomfortable. There, he is placed on a table while Glumdalclitch sits down on a stool beside him, with thirty people at a time walking through as he performs "tricks."

Gulliver is exhausted by the journey to the marketplace, but upon returning to the farmer's house, he finds that he is to be shown there as well. People come from miles around and are charged great sums to view him. Thinking that Gulliver can make him a great fortune, the farmer takes him and Glumdalclitch on a trip to the largest cities.

The three arrive in the largest city, Lorbrulgrud, and the farmer rents a room with a table for displaying Gulliver. By now, Gulliver can understand their language and speak it fairly well. He is shown ten times a day and pleases the visitors greatly.

ANALYSIS: PART II, CHAPTERS I–II

In Gulliver's adventure in Brobdingnag, many of the same issues that are brought up in the Lilliputian adventure are now brought up again, but this time Gulliver is in the exact opposite situation. Many of the jokes from Gulliver's adventure in Lilliput are played in reverse: instead of worrying about trampling on the Lilliputians, Gulliver is now at risk of being trampled upon; instead of being feared and admired for his gargantuan size, he is treated as a miniscule and insignificant curiosity; instead of displaying miniature livestock in England to make money, he is put on display for money by the farmer. As a whole, the second voyage serves to emphasize the importance of size and the relativity of human culture.

Gulliver's initial experiences with the Brobdingnagians are not positive. First they almost trample him, then the farmer virtually enslaves him, forcing him to perform tricks for paying spectators. This enslavement emphasizes the fundamental humanity of the Brobdingnagians—just like Europeans, they are happy to make a quick buck when the opportunity arises—and also makes concrete Gulliver's lowly status. Whereas in Lilliput, his size gives him almost godlike powers, allowing him to become a hero and a *Nardac* to the Lilliputian people, in Brobdingnag his different size has exactly the opposite effect. Even his small acts of heroism, like his battle against the rats, are seen by the Brobdingnagians as, at best, "tricks."

Swift continues to play with language in a way that both emphasizes his main satirical points about politics, ethics, and culture and makes fun of language itself. In the first few pages of this section, while Gulliver is still at sea, he describes in complicated naval jargon the various attempts his ship makes to deal with an oncoming storm. The rush of words is nearly incomprehensible, and it is meant to be so—the point is to satirize the jargon used by writers of travel books and sailing accounts, which in Swift's view was often overblown and ridiculous. By taking the tendency to use jargon to an extreme and putting it in the mouth of the gullible and straightforward Gulliver, Swift makes a mockery of those who would try to demonstrate their expertise through convoluted language. Attacks like this one, which are repeated elsewhere in the novel, are part of Swift's larger mission: to criticize the validity of various kinds of expert knowledge that are more showy than helpful, whether legal, naval, or, as in the third voyage, scientific.

PART II, CHAPTERS III–V

SUMMARY: CHAPTER III

The strain of traveling and performing "tricks" takes its toll on Gulliver, and he begins to grow very thin. The farmer notices Gulliver's condition and resolves to make as much money as possible before Gulliver dies. Meanwhile, an order comes from the court, commanding the farmer to bring Gulliver to the queen for her entertainment.

The queen is delighted with Gulliver's behavior and buys him from the farmer for 1,000 gold pieces. Gulliver requests that Glumdalclitch be allowed to live in the palace as well. Gulliver explains his suffering to the queen, and she is impressed by his intelligence. She takes him to the king, who at first thinks he is a mechanical creation. He sends for great scholars to observe Gulliver, and they decide that he is unfit for survival, since there is no way he could feed himself. Gulliver tries to explain that he comes from a country in which everything is in proportion to himself, but they do not seem to believe him.

Glumdalclitch is given an apartment in the palace and a governess to teach her, and special quarters are built for Gulliver out of a box. They also have clothes made for him from fine silk, but Gulliver finds them very cumbersome. The queen grows quite accustomed to his company, finding him very entertaining at dinner, especially when he cuts and eats his meat. He finds her way of eating repulsive, since her size allows her to swallow huge amounts of food in a single gulp.

The king converses with Gulliver on issues of politics, and laughs at his descriptions of the goings-on in Europe. He finds it amusing that people of such small stature should think themselves so important, and Gulliver is at first offended. He then comes to realize that he too has begun to think of his world as ridiculous.

The queen's dwarf is not happy with Gulliver, since he is used to being the smallest person in the palace and a source of diversion for the royal court. He drops Gulliver into a bowl of cream, but Gulliver is able to swim to safety and the dwarf is punished. At another point, the dwarf sticks Gulliver into a marrowbone, where he is forced to remain until someone pulls him out.

SUMMARY: CHAPTER IV

Gulliver describes the geography of Brobdingnag, noting first that since the land stretches out about 6,000 miles there must be a severe error in European maps. The kingdom is bounded on one side by mountains and on the other three sides by the sea. The water is so rough that there is no trade with other nations. The rivers are well stocked with giant fish, but the fish in the sea are of the same size as those in the rest of the world—and therefore not worth catching.

Gulliver is carried around the city in a special traveling-box, and people always crowd around to see him. He asks to see the largest temple in the country and is not overwhelmed by its size, since at a height of 3,000 feet it is proportionally smaller than the largest steeple in England.

SUMMARY: CHAPTER V

Gulliver is happy in Brobdingnag except for the many mishaps that befall him because of his diminutive size. In one unpleasant incident, the dwarf, angry at Gulliver for teasing him, shakes an apple tree over his head. One of the apples strikes Gulliver in the back and knocks him over. Another time, he is left outside during a hailstorm and is so bruised and battered that he cannot leave the house for ten days.

Gulliver and his nursemaid are often invited to the apartments of the ladies of the court, and there he is treated as a plaything of little significance. They enjoy stripping his clothes and placing him in their bosoms, and he is appalled by their strong smell, noting that a Lilliputian told him that he smelled quite repulsive to them. The women also strip their own clothes in front of him, and he finds their skin extremely ugly and uneven.

The queen orders a special boat to be built for Gulliver. The boat is placed in a cistern, and Gulliver rows in it for his own enjoyment and for the amusement of the queen and her court.

Yet another danger arises in the form of a monkey, which takes Gulliver up a ladder, holding him like a baby and force-feeding him. He is rescued from the monkey, and Glumdalclitch pries the food from his mouth with a needle, after which Gulliver vomits. He is so weak and bruised that he stays in bed for two weeks. The monkey is killed and orders are sent out that no other monkeys be kept in the palace.

ANALYSIS: PART II, CHAPTERS III–V

Gulliver's continued adventures in Brobdingnag serve to illustrate the importance of physical size. Reduced to a twelfth of the size of the people who surround him, Gulliver finds all of his pride and importance withering away. Without physical power to back him up—whether the normal level that he experiences in England or the extraordinary level of his time in Lilliput—it is impossible for Gulliver to maintain the illusion of his own importance.

These chapters contain, in addition to the continuing satire of European culture, some of the most entertaining portions of the novel. Gulliver is treated like a doll, tormented by the court dwarf, and adopted, briefly, by a monkey. For the most part, these scenes serve to hammer home the image of Gulliver's miniscule size as compared to the Brobdingnagians, but they also achieve several more significant accomplishments. The conflict with the dwarf is a good example of such a point. The dwarf, unable to gain the power that generally accompanies great physical size, has tried to make a place for himself in society by capitalizing instead on the distinctive lack of power that accompanies his tiny size. When Gulliver enters the court, he challenges the dwarf's distinctiveness, and the dwarf responds aggressively. If there is a moral to the episode, it is that the politics of those who attempt to achieve power not through physical strength but through their distinctiveness can be just as immoral as the mainstream.

Another key episode takes place with Gulliver's visit to the ladies of the court. The fantasy of domination and submission—realized when Gulliver becomes the sexual plaything of the ladies—is overshadowed by his outright disgust at their smell and appearance. He knows, theoretically, that if he were their size they would be just as attractive as the well-pampered court ladies of England, but since he is not, their flaws are literally magnified, and they appear to him malodorous, blemished, and crude. Swift's point is that anything, even the smoothest skin or the most appealing political system, has imperfections, and these imperfections are bound to be exposed under close enough scrutiny. In a sense, what looks perfect to us is not actually perfect—it is simply not imperfect enough for our limited senses to notice.

At the time that Swift was writing *Gulliver's Travels,* however, technology that could accentuate these imperfect senses was burgeoning, and Gulliver's microscopic view of flies and flesh may be a reference to the relatively recent discovery of the microscope. The late seventeenth century saw the first publication of books containing magnified images illustrating that various items—fleas, hair, skin—contained details and flaws that had previously been hidden. Gulliver lives this microscopic experience directly. In a magnified world, everything takes on new levels of complexity and imperfection, demonstrating that the truth about objects is heavily influenced by the observer's perspective.

Part II, Chapters VI–VIII

Summary: Chapter VI

> *He said, he knew no Reason, why those who entertain*
> *Opinions prejudicial to the Publick, should be obliged*
> *to change, or should not be obliged to conceal them.*
> (See QUOTATIONS, p. 60)

Gulliver makes himself a comb from the stumps of hair left after the king has been shaved. He also collects hairs from the king and uses them to weave the backs of two small chairs, which he gives to the queen as curiosities. Gulliver is brought to a musical performance, but it is so loud that he can hardly make it out. Gulliver decides to play the spinet for the royal family, but must contrive a novel way to do it, since the instrument is so big. He uses large sticks and runs over the keyboard with them, but he can still strike only sixteen keys.

Thinking that the king has unjustly come to regard England as insignificant and laughable, Gulliver tries to tell him more about England, describing the government and culture there. The king

asks many questions and is particularly struck by the violence of
the history Gulliver describes. He then takes Gulliver into his hand
and, explaining that he finds the world that Gulliver describes to be
ridiculous, contemptuous, and strange, tells him that he concludes
that most Englishmen sound like "odious Vermin."

> I cannot but conclude the Bulk of your Natives, to be
> the most pernicious Race of little odious Vermin that
> Nature ever suffered to crawl upon the Surface of the
> Earth.
>
> (See QUOTATIONS, p. 61)

SUMMARY: CHAPTER VII

Gulliver is disturbed by the king's evaluation of England. He tries
to tell him about gunpowder, describing it as a great invention and
offering it to the king as a gesture of friendship. The king is appalled
by the proposal, and Gulliver is taken aback, thinking that the king
has refused a great opportunity. He thinks that the king is unneces-
sarily scrupulous and narrow-minded for not being more open to
the inventions of Gulliver's world.

Gulliver finds the people of Brobdingnag in general to be ignorant
and poorly educated. Their laws are not allowed to exceed in words
the number of letters in their alphabet, and no arguments may be
written about them. They know the art of printing but do not have
many books, and their writing is simple and straightforward. One
text describes the insignificance and weakness of Brobdingnagians
and even argues that at one point they must have been much larger.

SUMMARY: CHAPTER VIII

Gulliver wants to recover his freedom. The king orders any small
ship to be brought to the city, hoping that they might find a woman
with whom Gulliver can propagate. Gulliver fears that any offspring thus produced would be kept in cages or given to the nobility
as pets. He has been in Brobdingnag for two years and wants to be
among his own kind again.

Gulliver is taken to the south coast, and both Glumdalclitch and
Gulliver fall ill. Gulliver says that he wants fresh air, and a page carries him out to the shore in his traveling-box. He asks to be left to
sleep in his hammock, and the boy wanders off. An eagle grabs hold
of Gulliver's box and flies off with him, and then suddenly Gulliver
feels himself falling and lands in the water. He worries that he will
drown or starve to death, but then feels the box being pulled. He

hears a voice telling him that his box is tied to a ship and that a carpenter will come to drill a hole in the top. Gulliver says that they can simply use a finger to pry it open, and he hears laughter. He realizes that he is speaking to people of his own height and climbs a ladder out of his box and onto their ship.

Gulliver begins to recover on the ship, and he tries to tell the sailors the story of his recent journey. He shows them things he saved from Brobdingnag, like his comb and a tooth pulled from a footman. He has trouble adjusting to the sailors' small size, and he finds himself shouting all the time. When he reaches home, it takes him some time to grow accustomed to his old life, and his wife asks him to never go to sea again.

ANALYSIS: PART II, CHAPTERS VI–VIII

In the previous section, Gulliver's personal insignificance is illustrated by his reduction to the status of a plaything in the court. In this section, the same lesson is repeated on a larger scale when he describes the culture and politics of Europe to the king of Brobdingnag. Suddenly, all of the life-and-death issues that seemed so important when Gulliver was in Europe are revealed to be the trivial conflicts of miniscule people. They are not only insignificant, but the king also derides them as "odious." In his eyes, the tiny size of the Europeans is matched by their moral weakness. Gulliver's long discussions with the king leave him feeling humiliated.

Nonetheless, Gulliver manages to maintain some sense of the importance of England in the face of the king's criticisms. But his protests seem so transparently groundless that each argument he gives for England's superiority, including his argument that the king is too dull-witted to see the beauty of English culture, serves only to emphasize the futility of his resistance. In the end, the king's assessment of the Europeans as "odious vermin" wins the day. Gulliver's personality plays an important role in pushing this satirical point home. His naïveté, his gullibility, and his ingenuous praise for England all accentuate his similarity to the Lilliputians: convinced of his own significance, he is unable to realize the pettiness and imperfection of the society he represents.

This imperfection is not just one of organization or law. If that were the only problem with English society as Swift saw it, then *Gulliver's Travels* would have been a much more boring and less significant work. The imperfection, rather, is fundamentally one of morals: the British, and by extension humanity in general, are not only bad at getting what they want, they also want bad things. This truth is illustrated in Gulliver's offer of the secret of gunpowder to the king. The king refuses without a second thought, not because the Brobdingnagians have superior technology, but because he is horrified by the potential moral and physical consequences of gunpowder. Most preindustrial societies would treat gunpowder as an achievement of high order. But the king indicates that he feels it would be better to live where violence and destruction are minimized instead of exaggerated. Gulliver's inability to understand the king's position—he sees the refusal as a weakness in the king's understanding—illustrates how the values of a violent society are deeply ingrained in Gulliver. Observing both the king and Gulliver, we are invited to choose between them.

Nevertheless, the Brobdingnagians are not perfect, however much more developed their moral sense may be than Gulliver's. They are, rather, humans who have achieved a gargantuan level of moral achievement. Unlike the petty and miniscule Lilliputians, in whom the human vices of pride and self-righteousness are exaggerated, the Brobdingnagians have constructed a society in which those vices are minimized as much as possible. They still exist—for instance, the farmer exploits Gulliver by showing him off for profit—but they are not, as they are in England, encoded in the structure of government itself. The Brobdingnagians—more moral than the Lilliputians, more practical than the Laputans of the third voyage, and more human than the Houyhnhnms of the fourth voyage—are in some ways the most admirable of the societies Gulliver encounters.

PART III, CHAPTERS I–III

SUMMARY: CHAPTER I

Gulliver has been home in England only ten days when a visitor comes to his house, asking him to sail aboard his ship in two months' time. Gulliver agrees and prepares to set out for the East Indies. On the voyage, pirates attack the ship. Gulliver hears a Dutch voice among them and speaks to the pirate in Dutch, begging to be set free since he and the pirate are both Christians. A Japanese pirate tells them they will not die, and Gulliver tells the Dutchman that he is surprised to find more mercy in a heathen than in a Christian. The Dutchman grows angry and punishes Gulliver by sending him out to sea in a small boat with only four days' worth of food.

Gulliver finds some islands and goes ashore on one of them. He sets up camp but then notices something strange: the sun is mysteriously obscured for some time. He then sees a landmass dropping down from the sky and notices that it is crawling with people. He is baffled by this floating island and shouts up to its inhabitants. They lower the island and send down a chain by which he is drawn up.

SUMMARY: CHAPTER II

Gulliver is immediately surrounded by people and notices that they are all quite odd. Their heads are all tilted to one side or the other, with one eye turned inward and the other looking up. Their clothes are adorned with images of celestial bodies and musical instruments. Some of the people are servants, and each of them carries a "flapper" made of a stick with a pouch tied to the end. Their job is to aid conversation by striking the ear of the listener and the mouth of the speaker at the appropriate times to prevent their masters' minds from wandering off.

Gulliver is conveyed to the king, who sits behind a table loaded with mathematical instruments. They wait an hour before there is some opportunity to arouse the king from his thoughts, at which point he is struck with the flapper. The king says something, and Gulliver's ear is struck with the flapper as well, even though he tries to explain that he does not require such actions. It becomes clear that he and the king cannot speak any of the same languages, so Gulliver is taken to an apartment and served dinner.

A teacher is sent to instruct Gulliver in the language of the island, and he is able to learn several sentences. He discovers that the name of the island is Laputa, which in their language means "floating island." A tailor is also sent to provide him with new clothes, and while he is waiting for these clothes, the king orders the island to be moved. It is taken to a point above the capital city of the kingdom, Lagado, passing villages along the way and collecting petitions from the king's subjects by means of ropes sent down to the lands below.

The language of the Laputans relies heavily on mathematical and musical concepts, as they value these theoretical disciplines above everything. The Laputans despise practical geometry, thinking it vulgar—so much so that they make sure that there are no right angles in their buildings. They are very good with charts and figures but very clumsy in practical matters. They practice astrology and dread changes in the celestial bodies.

SUMMARY: CHAPTER III

The island is exactly circular and consists of 10,000 acres of land. At the center there is a cave for astronomers, containing all their instruments and a lodestone six yards long. It moves the island with its magnetic force, since it has two charges that can be reversed by means of an attached control. The mineral that acts upon the magnet is large enough to allow it to move only over the country directly beneath it. When the king wants to punish a particular region of the country, he can keep the island above it, depriving the lands below of sun and rain. Such measures failed to work in one town, where the rebellious inhabitants had stored provisions of food in advance. They planned to force the island to come so low that it would be trapped forever and to kill the king and his officials in order to take over the government. Instead, the king ordered the island to stop descending and gave in to the town's demands. The king is not allowed to leave the floating island, nor is his family.

ANALYSIS: PART III, CHAPTERS I–III

Gulliver's third voyage is more scattered than the others, involving stops at Laputa, Balnibarbi, Glubbdubdrib, Luggnagg, and Japan. Swift completed the account of this voyage after that of the fourth voyage was already written, and there are hints that it was assembled from notes that Swift had made for an earlier satire of abstract knowledge. Nonetheless, it plays a crucial role in the novel as a whole. Whereas the first two voyages are mostly satires of politics and ethics, the third voyage extends Swift's attack to science, learning, and abstract thought, offering a critique of excessive rationalism, or reliance on theory, during the Enlightenment.

Laputa is more complex than Lilliput or Brobdingnag because its strangeness is not based on differences of size but, instead, on the primacy of abstract theoretical concerns over concrete practical concerns in Laputan culture. Nonetheless, physical power is just as important in Laputa as it is in Lilliput and Brobdingnag. Here, power is exercised not through physical size but through technology. The government floats over the rest of the kingdom, using technology to gain advantage over its subjects. The floating island is both a formidable weapon and an allegorical image that represents the distance between the government and the people it governs. The king is oblivious to the real concerns of the people below—indeed, he has never even *been* below. The nobility and scientific thinkers of the island are similarly far removed from the people and their concerns, so much so that they need to be aroused from their thoughts and daydreams by their servants. The need to regulate when people listen and when they talk by means of such intermediaries as the servants with their flappers is absurd, and the mechanized quality of this system demonstrates how nonhuman these people are. Indeed, abstract theory dominates all aspects of Laputan life, from language to architecture to geography. We are compelled to wonder whether the Laputans' rigid adherence to such principles—their disdain for practical geometry, for example, leads them to renounce right angles—limits their society.

Swift continues to satirize specialized language in his description of the technique used to move the island from one place to another. The method of assigning letters to parts of a mechanism and then describing the movement of these parts from one point to another resembles the mechanistic philosophical and scientific descriptions of Swift's time. The use of this technique does nothing but obscure what Gulliver is trying to say, but he is so enamored of its supposed geometrical rigor that he uses it to excess, as he does earlier with naval language.

PART III, CHAPTERS IV–XI

SUMMARY: CHAPTER IV

Gulliver feels neglected on Laputa, since the inhabitants seem interested only in mathematics and music and are far superior to him in their knowledge. He is bored by their conversation and wants to leave. There is one lord of the court whom Gulliver finds to be intelligent and curious, but who is regarded by the other inhabitants of Laputa as stupid because he has no ear for music. Gulliver asks this lord to petition the king to let him leave the island. The petition succeeds, and he is let down on the mountains above Lagado. He visits another lord, named Munodi, and is invited to stay at his home.

Gulliver and Munodi visit a nearby town, which Gulliver finds to be populated by poorly-dressed inhabitants living in shabby houses. The soil is badly cultivated and the people appear miserable. They then travel to Munodi's country house, first passing many barren fields but then arriving in a lush green area that Munodi says belongs to his estate. He says that the other lords criticize him heavily for the "mismanagement" of his land.

Munodi explains that forty years ago some people went to Laputa and returned with new ideas about mathematics and art.

They decided to establish an academy in Lagado to develop new theories on agriculture and construction and to initiate projects to improve the lives of the city's inhabitants. However, the theories have never produced any results and the new techniques have left the country in ruin. He encourages Gulliver to visit the academy, which Gulliver is glad to do since he was once intrigued by projects of this sort himself.

SUMMARY: CHAPTER V

Gulliver visits the academy, where he meets a man engaged in a project to extract sunbeams from cucumbers. He also meets a scientist trying to turn excrement back into food. Another is attempting to turn ice into gunpowder and is writing a treatise about the malleability of fire, hoping to have it published. An architect is designing a way to build houses from the roof down, and a blind master is teaching his blind apprentices to mix colors for painters according to smell and touch. An agronomist is designing a method of plowing fields with hogs by first burying food in the ground and then letting the hogs loose to dig it out. A doctor in another room tries to cure patients by blowing air through them. Gulliver leaves him trying to revive a dog that he has killed by supposedly curing it in this way.

On the other side of the academy there are people engaged in speculative learning. One professor has a class full of boys working from a machine that produces random sets of words. Using this machine, the teacher claims, anyone can write a book on philosophy or politics. A linguist in another room is attempting to remove all the elements of language except nouns. Such pruning, he claims, would make language more concise and prolong lives, since every word spoken is detrimental to the human body. Since nouns are only things, furthermore, it would be even easier to carry things and never speak at all. Another professor tries to teach mathematics by having his students eat wafers that have mathematical proofs written on them.

SUMMARY: CHAPTER VI

Gulliver then visits professors who are studying issues of government. One claims that women should be taxed according to their beauty and skill at dressing, and another claims that conspiracies against the government could be discovered by studying the excrement of subjects. Gulliver grows tired of the academy and begins to yearn for a return to England.

SUMMARY: CHAPTER VII

Gulliver tries to travel to Luggnagg, but he finds no ship available. Since he has to wait a month, he is advised to take a trip to Glubbdubdrib, the island of magicians. Gulliver visits the governor of Glubbdubdrib, and he finds that servants who appear and disappear like spirits attend the governor. The governor tells Gulliver that he has the power to call up any shade he would like. Gulliver chooses Alexander the Great, who assures him that he died not from poison but from excessive drinking. He then sees the Carthaginian general Hannibal and the Roman leaders Caesar, Pompey, and Brutus.

SUMMARY: CHAPTER VIII

Gulliver sets apart one day to speak with the most venerated people in history, starting with Homer and Aristotle. He asks the French philosophers René Descartes and Pierre Gassendi to describe their systems to Aristotle, who freely acknowledges his own mistakes while pointing out that systems of nature will always vary from age to age.

SUMMARY: CHAPTER IX

Gulliver then returns to Luggnagg, where he is confined despite his desire to return to England. He is ordered to appear at the king's court and is given lodging and an allowance. He learns that subjects are expected to lick the floor as they approach the king, and that the king sometimes gets rid of opponents in the court by coating the floor with poison.

SUMMARY: CHAPTER X

The Luggnaggians tell Gulliver about certain immortal people, children born with a red spot on their foreheads who are called Struldbrugs. Gulliver devises a whole system of what he would do if he were immortal, starting with the acquisition of riches and knowledge. Contrary to his fantasy, however, he is told that after the age of thirty, most Struldbrugs grow sad and dejected, and by eighty, they are incapable of affection and envious of those who are able to die. If two of the Struldbrugs marry, the marriage is dissolved when one reaches eighty, because "those who are condemned without any fault of their own to a perpetual continuance in the world should not have their misery doubled by the load of a wife." He meets some of these people and finds them to be unhappy and unpleasant, and he regrets ever wishing for their state.

SUMMARY: CHAPTER XI

Gulliver is finally able to depart from Luggnagg, after refusing employment there, and he arrives safely in Japan. From there he gains passage on a Dutch ship by pretending to be from Holland and sets sail from Amsterdam to England, where he finds his family in good health.

ANALYSIS: PART III, CHAPTERS IV–XI

Swift continues his mockery of academia by describing the projects carried out in the cities below Laputa. The academy serves to create entirely useless projects while the people starve outside its walls. Each project described, such as the extraction of sunbeams from a cucumber, is not only impossibly flawed but also purposeless. Even if its scientific foundations were correct, it would still serve no real purpose for the people meant to gain from it. The result is a society in which science is promoted for no real reason and time is wasted as a matter of course.

Much of Swift's inspiration for the scientists in this voyage came from the Royal Society of London for the Improving of Natural Knowledge, a scientific society founded in 1660 that had an important effect on the development of science in Europe. The prominent early scientists Robert Boyle, Robert Hooke, and Isaac Newton were all members of the Royal Society. All of them, but particularly Newton, were influential promoters of scientific theories that were at the heart of the Scientific Revolution. The Royal Society assigned itself the task of using the new techniques of science to improve the crafts, but it was far more successful at discovering natural phenomena than it was at building new, useful technologies. As a result, the Royal Society was open to the parody created by Swift, in which absentminded philosophers ruin a country by forcing its people to follow their novel and wholly useless methods. Interestingly, most of the experiments parodied by Swift had actually been proposed or carried out by British scientists at the time of his writing.

Glubbdubdrib offers the opportunity for Swift to satirize various historical figures, undermining their images as paragons of virtue or learning. Gulliver's interaction with the dead hearkens back to Dante Alighieri's fourteenth-century poem *Inferno,* in which Dante himself travels through the various regions of hell and witnesses sinners being punished. This imaginary tour of hell allowed Dante the author to skewer his political opponents and enemies, just as Swift's imaginary wanderings allow him to ridicule certain aspects of society. Gulliver's visit to Glubbdubdrib is part of Swift's attempt in the third voyage to undercut standards of abstract learning. At the same time, however, Swift does elevate certain people above others. Generally speaking, the ancient Greeks and Romans are held up as truly virtuous, whereas the Europeans who have lived since are held up as somewhat degenerate.

The Struldbrugs of Luggnagg provide an opportunity for Swift to satirize human desires. Many would seek eternal life, and the primary benefit of old age, as Gulliver sees it, is the ability to use one's accumulated wisdom to help humanity. The reality is much less glorious—instead of growing in wisdom, the immortal Struldbrugs grow only more prejudiced and selfish, eventually becoming a detriment to the whole Luggnaggian society. Furthermore, the Struldbrugs' immense sadness despite their seeming advantage shows the emptiness of Gulliver's desire—a desire prominent in Western society—to acquire riches. Swift denounces such self-absorbed goals as the province of small minds unconcerned with the good of society as a whole.

Part IV, Chapters I–IV

Summary: Chapter I

Gulliver stays home for five months, but he then leaves his pregnant wife to set sail again, this time as the captain of a ship called the *Adventure*. Many of his sailors die of illness, so he recruits more along the way. His crewmembers mutiny under the influence of these new sailors and become pirates. Gulliver is left on an unknown shore, after being confined to his cabin for several days. In the distance, he sees animals with long hair, goatlike beards, and sharp claws, which they use to climb trees. Gulliver decides that these animals are extremely ugly and sets forth to find settlers, but he encounters one of the animals on his way.

Gulliver takes out his sword and hits the animal with the flat side of it. The animal roars loudly, and a herd of others like it attack Gulliver by attempting to defecate on him. He hides, but then he sees them hurrying away. He emerges from his hiding place to see that the beasts have been scared away by a horse. The horse observes Gulliver carefully, and then it neighs in a complicated cadence. Another horse joins the first and the two seem to be involved in a discussion. Gulliver tries to leave, but one of the horses calls him back.

The horses appear to be so intelligent that Gulliver concludes that they are magicians who have transformed themselves into horses. He addresses them directly and asks to be taken to a house or village. The horses use the words "Yahoo" and "Houyhnhnm," which Gulliver tries to pronounce.

SUMMARY: CHAPTER II

Gulliver is led to a house, and he takes out gifts, expecting to meet people. He finds instead that there are more horses in the house, sitting down and engaged in various activities. He thinks that the house belongs to a person of great importance, and he wonders why they should have horses for servants. A horse looks Gulliver over and says the word "Yahoo." Gulliver is led out to the courtyard, where a few of the ugly creatures Gulliver has seen are tied up. Gulliver is lined up and compared with one of the creatures, and Gulliver finds that the creature does look quite human. The horses test Gulliver by offering him various foods: hay, which he refuses, and flesh, which he finds repulsive but which the Yahoo devours. The horses determine that he likes milk and give him large amounts of it to drink.

Another horse comes to dine, and they all take great pleasure in teaching Gulliver to pronounce words in their language. They cannot determine what he might like to eat until Gulliver suggests that he could make bread from their oats. He is given a place to sleep with straw for the time being.

SUMMARY: CHAPTER III

Gulliver endeavors to learn the horses' language, and they are impressed by his intellect and curiosity. After three months, he can answer most of their questions and tries to explain that he comes from across the sea, but the horses, or Houyhnhnms, do not believe that such a thing is possible. They think that Gulliver is some kind of Yahoo, though superior to the rest of his species. He asks them to stop using that word to refer to him, and they consent.

SUMMARY: CHAPTER IV

Gulliver tries to explain that the Yahoos are the governing creatures where he comes from, and the Houyhnhnms ask how their horses are employed. Gulliver explains that they are used for traveling, racing, and drawing chariots, and the Houyhnhnms express disbelief that anything as weak as a Yahoo would dare to mount a horse that was so much stronger than it. Gulliver explains that the horses are trained from a young age to be tame and obedient. He describes the state of humanity in Europe and is asked to speak more specifically of his own country.

ANALYSIS: PART IV, CHAPTERS I–IV

In the fourth voyage, Gulliver reaches a stage at which he no longer cares for humankind at all, though in this section we see only the beginnings of his transformation. After visiting countries in which he is too large, too small, and too down-to-earth, he finds himself in a country where he is neither rational nor moral enough, stuck in the limbo between the humane Houyhnhnms and the untamed, unruly Yahoos. In these chapters we see the rough outline of Houyhnhnm society, which Gulliver finds pleasant but still alien. In the next section, he attempts to become a part of this society.

In the meantime, we are treated to a description of the Houyhnhnms' society. Swift plays a clever trick in the first two chapters, obscuring the true nature of the Houyhnhnms so that we follow Gulliver in his mistaken belief that the horses are magicians or the servants of a magician. Instead of telling us outright that the horses are intelligent, Swift allows us to discover this fact through Gulliver's eyes. As a result, what looks strange to Gulliver also looks strange to us, and at some point in the description of the horses' behavior, we realize that there is nothing more to these creatures than meets the eye. Instead of being tools of humans, the horses are revealed to be intelligent in their own right. In one stroke, they go from being a manifestation of humanity to something utterly nonhuman.

There are a number of differences between the first three voyages and the fourth. Three of these differences are particularly important because they signal changes in the overall satirical thrust of the novel: Gulliver finds himself not among fellow humans, however distorted in size or culture, but among a race of horses; instead of being happy to leave, he is eager to stay; and instead of seeing the world through his eyes, we are forced to step back and look at Gulliver himself as an important, though not always sympathetic, player in the drama.

In other ways, these chapters are similar to the initial chapters of the other voyages. Gulliver arrives in a strange land, becomes the guest or prisoner of the people who live there, learns their language, and slowly begins to learn about their culture and tell them about European culture. The major difference here is that the humans, or

Yahoos, are not his hosts. Instead, they are vile creatures that get nothing but his contempt. In his descriptions of the Yahoos, Swift uses the technique of describing the familiar in unfamiliar terms. Only slowly does it dawn on us that the Yahoos are humans. As with the realization that the Houyhnhnms are intelligent in their own right, the sudden shock—which we experience along with Gulliver—of recognizing the Yahoos for what they are strengthens the impact of the description.

PART IV, CHAPTERS V–XII

SUMMARY: CHAPTER V
Over the course of two years, Gulliver describes the state of affairs in Europe, speaking to his Houyhnhnm master about the English Revolution and the war with France. He is asked to explain the causes of war, and he does his best to provide reasons. He is also asked to speak of law and the justice system, which he does in some detail, criticizing lawyers severely in the process.

SUMMARY: CHAPTER VI
The discussion then turns to other topics, such as money and the different kinds of food eaten in Europe. Gulliver explains the different occupations in which people are involved, including service professions such as medicine and construction.

SUMMARY: CHAPTER VII
Gulliver develops such a love for the Houyhnhnms that he no longer desires to return to humankind. His master tells him that he has considered all of Gulliver's claims about his home country and has come to the conclusion that Gulliver's people are not so different from the Yahoos as they may at first have seemed. He describes all the flaws of the Yahoos, principally detailing their greed and selfishness. He admits that Gulliver's humans have different systems of learning, law, government, and art but says that their natures are not different from those of the Yahoos.

SUMMARY: CHAPTER VIII
Gulliver wants to observe the similarities between Yahoos and humans for himself, so he asks to go among the Yahoos. He finds them to be very nimble from infancy but unable to learn anything. They are strong, cowardly, and malicious.

The principle virtues of the Houyhnhnms are their friendship and benevolence. They are concerned more with the community than with their own personal advantages, even choosing their mates so as to promote the race as a whole. They breed industriousness, cleanliness, and civility in their young and exercise them for speed and strength.

Summary: Chapter IX

Gulliver's master attends a Grand Assembly of Houyhnhnms, where the horses debate whether or not to extinguish the Yahoos from the face of the Earth. Gulliver's master suggests that instead of killing them, they should, as the Europeans do with their horses, merely castrate them. Eventually, unable to breed, the Yahoos will die out, and in the meantime the Houyhnhnms can breed asses to take their place.

Gulliver then describes further aspects of the Houyhnhnms' society. They create excellent poetry, have a sound knowledge of medicinal herbs, build simple houses, and usually live about seventy or seventy-five years, dying of old age. They feel no sorrow about death, accepting it as a routine element of life. They have no writing system and no word to express anything evil.

Summary: Chapter X

A room is made for Gulliver, and he furnishes it well. He also makes new clothes for himself and settles into life with the Houyhnhnms quite easily. He begins to think of his friends and family back home as Yahoos. However, he is called by his master and told that others have taken offense at his being kept in the house as a Houyhnhnm. The master has no choice but to ask Gulliver to leave. Gulliver is very upset to hear that he is to be banished. He builds a canoe with the help of a fellow-servant and departs sadly.

Summary: Chapter XI

Gulliver does not want to return to Europe, and so he begins to search for an island where he can live as he likes. He finds land and discovers natives there. He is struck by an arrow and tries to escape the natives' darts by paddling out to sea. He sees a sail in the distance and thinks of going toward it, but then decides he would rather live with the barbarians than the European Yahoos, so he hides from the ship. The seamen, including Don Pedro de Mendez, discover him after landing near his hiding place. They question him, laughing at his strange horselike manner of speaking, and cannot understand his desire to escape from their ship. Don Pedro treats Gulliver hospitably, offering him food, drink, and clothes, but Gulliver can think of him only as a Yahoo and is thus repulsed by him.

Gulliver is forced to travel back to England, where he returns to his family, which has been convinced that he is dead. He is filled with disgust and contempt for them. For a year he cannot stand to be near his wife and children, and he buys two horses and converses with them for four hours each day.

SUMMARY: CHAPTER XII

> *Here commences a New Dominion . . . the Earth*
> *reeking with the Blood of its Inhabitants.*
> *(See* QUOTATIONS, *p. 62)*

Gulliver concludes his narrative by acknowledging that the law requires him to report his findings to the government but that he can see no military advantage in attacking any of the locations he discovered. Moreover, he particularly wishes to protect the Houyhnhnms.

> *[W]hen I behold a Lump of Deformity . . . it*
> *immediately breaks all the Measures of my Patience.*
> *(See* QUOTATIONS, *p. 62)*

ANALYSIS: PART IV, CHAPTERS V–XII

The desire that Gulliver experiences to live among the animals persists in European literature. This desire is echoed later by the Romantics, who, writing in the nineteenth century, idealized pastoral simplicity and a return to nature. In the case of the Romantics, however, this love of nature was a response to the urbanization and industrialization of European society. In Swift's case, the return to nature is a two-pronged tool for satire, skewering both human civilization itself and those who would look to animals for a model of how to live.

For the first time, Gulliver finds himself wanting to stay in exile from humanity, but he is not given the choice. He is appalled by the idea of going to live among the Yahoos, and he has so fully adopted the belief system of the Houyhnhnms that he cannot help but see his wife and children as primitive, ugly, beastlike creatures. But at the same time, he realizes that he has been living with the Houyhnhnms on borrowed time, pretending only half-successfully to be as rational as they are. The simplicity of the Houyhnhnms' world attracts him, but it is not a world in which he is allowed to live. In the end, he is forced to return to the world from which he came—a single world that encompasses all of the flaws and complexities he has encountered in his travels. But even there Gulliver cannot rest easy. Having seen the things he has, the world of Yahoos is contemptible and disgusting to him. Barely able to tolerate the presence of his family, he retreats into a kind of madness, spending his days talking to the horses in his stable as if to recreate the idyll of Houyhnhnmland.

In the first three voyages, it is easy to identify with Gulliver, but in the last voyage he becomes so alienated from humanity that it is difficult to sympathize with him. This shift in our loyalty is accompanied by a shift in the method of satire. Whereas in the first voyages we can look through Gulliver's eyes—sharing his astonishment at the Lilliputians' miniature society, his discomfort at being the plaything of the Brobdingnagian giants, and his contempt for the tyrannical intellectualism of the Laputans—here, in the fourth voyage, we are forced to step back and look not with Gulliver, but at him.

Although in some ways the Houyhnhnms are the ideal for which Gulliver strives unsuccessfully among his fellow humans, in another way they are just as much the victims of Swift's satire as the peoples of the first three voyages. Paragons of virtue and rationality, the horses are also dull, simple, and lifeless. Their language is impoverished, their mating loveless, and their understanding of the complex play of social forces naïve. What is missing in the horses is exactly that which makes human life rich: the complicated interplay of selfishness, altruism, love, hate, and all other emotions. In other words, the Houyhnhnms' society is perfect for Houyhnhnms, but it is hopeless for humans. Houyhnhnm society is, in stark contrast to the societies of the first three voyages, devoid of all that is human.

IMPORTANT QUOTATIONS EXPLAINED

1. My Father had a small Estate in Nottinghamshire; I was
    the Third of five Sons. . . . I was bound Apprentice to Mr.
    James Bates, an eminent Surgeon in London . . . my Father
    now and then sending me small Sums of Money. . . . When
    I left Mr. Bates, I went down to my Father; where, by
    the Assistance of him and my Uncle John . . . I got Forty
    Pounds, and a Promise of Thirty Pounds a Year.

This introductory paragraph from Part I, Chapter I, is often passed over as simply providing the preliminary facts of Gulliver's life, the bare essentials needed in order to proceed to the more interesting travel narrative. But this introduction is deeply significant in its own right, and it reveals much about Gulliver's character that is necessary to understand not just his journeys but also his way of narrating them. Gulliver is bourgeois: he is primarily interested in money, acquisitions, and achievement, and his life story is filtered through these desires. The first sentence means more than just a statement of his financial situation, since the third son of a possessor of only a "small Estate" would have no hopes of inheriting enough on which to support himself and would be expected to leave the estate and seek his own fortune. If Gulliver had been the first-born son, he might very well not have embarked on his travels. But the passage is even more revealing in its tone, which is starkly impersonal. Gulliver provides no sentimental characterization of his father, Bates, or Uncle John; they appear in his story only insofar as they further him in life. There is no mention of any youthful dreams or ambitions or of any romantic attachments. This lack of an emotional inner life is traceable throughout his narrative until his virtual nervous breakdown at the very end.

2. He said, he knew no Reason, why those who entertain
   Opinions prejudicial to the Publick, should be obliged to
   change, or should not be obliged to conceal them. And, as
   it was Tyranny in any Government to require the first, so it
   was Weakness not to enforce the second.

This quotation comes from a conversation between Gulliver and
the king of Brobdingnag, in Part II, Chapter VI. The belief
expressed by the king is one that Swift, writing in his own
voice, expressed elsewhere: that people have the right to their own
beliefs but not the right to express them at will. As always, it is difficult to determine whether or not Swift's view is exactly the one
advanced by his characters. The king has little sympathy for many
English institutions as Gulliver describes them to him. Swift would
probably not have rejected such in-stitutions, and we should keep in
mind that Brobdingnagian criticism does not always imply Swiftian
criticism. Indeed, *Gulliver's Travels* could be considered to contain
at least a few "Opinions prejudicial to the Publick"—unpopular
opinions, in other words—so it is unlikely that Swift is in favor of
suppressing all social criticism entirely. Whatever the final interpretation, the quotation raises interesting issues of censorship, freedom
of speech, and the rightful place of indirect forms of criticism, such
as the satire of which Swift was a master.

3. My little Friend Grildrig. . . . I cannot but conclude the
   Bulk of your Natives, to be the most pernicious Race of
   little odious Vermin that Nature ever suffered to crawl
   upon the Surface of the Earth.

This famous judgment by the king of Brobdingnag on the people of
England, given in Part II, Chapter VI, after Gulliver (or "Grildrig")
has summarized the institutions of his native land, is a harsh denun-
ciation of mankind in its current state, and it stokes the misanthropy
that dominates Gulliver's mind by the end of *Gulliver's Travels*. The
judgment is particularly ironic because Gulliver's own purpose in
telling the king about England is to convince him of England's significance. The king acts as though Gulliver has intended to "clearly
prove" the faults of his land, though of course Gulliver does not
mean to make such an attack at all. Gulliver's speech on his country is not meant to be in the least critical, but it is received by the
king as a forceful damnation, so what is mocked here is not just

England but also Gulliver's naïve and unthinking acceptance of his own society. Swift subtly raises the issue of ideology, which refers to a person's brainwashed way of taking for granted a social arrangement that could or should be criticized and improved.

4. [T]hey go on Shore to rob and plunder; they see an harmless People, are entertained with Kindness, they give the Country a new Name, they take formal Possession of it for the King, they set up a rotten Plank or a Stone for a Memorial, they murder two or three Dozen of the Natives, bring away a Couple more by Force for a Sample, return home, and get their Pardon. Here commences a New Dominion acquired with a Title by Divine Right . . . the Earth reeking with the Blood of its Inhabitants.

This quotation comes from Part IV, Chapter XII, when Gulliver, having returned home to England after his stay among the Houyhnhnms, tries to apologize for what he sees as the only fault he committed while on his journeys: failing to claim the lands he visited in the name of England. First, he justifies his failure by saying that the countries he visited would not be worth the effort of conquering them. In the section quoted above, however, he goes even further by criticizing the practice of colonization itself. His picture of colonization as a criminal enterprise justified by the state for the purposes of trade and military power is one that looks familiar to modern eyes but was radical for Swift's time. Others criticized aspects of colonialism, such as the murder or enslavement of indigenous peoples, but few failed to see it as the justifiable expansion of purportedly civilized cultures. Swift employs his standard satirical technique here, as he first describes something without naming it in order to create an image in our minds, then gives it the name of something different, provoking us to rethink old assumptions.

5. My Reconcilement to the Yahoo-kind in general might
    not be so difficult, if they would be content with those
    Vices and Follies only which Nature hath entitled them
    to. I am not in the least provoked at the Sight of a Lawyer,
    a Pick-pocket, a Colonel. . . . This is all according to the
    due Course of Things: But, when I behold a Lump of
    Deformity, and Diseases both in Body and Mind, smitten
    with Pride, it immediately breaks all the Measures of my
    Patience; neither shall I ever be able to comprehend how
    such an Animal and such a Vice could tally together.

This quotation comes from the end of the narrative, in Part IV, Chapter XII, when Gulliver describes the difficulties he has had in readjusting to his own human culture. He now associates English and European culture with the Yahoos, though the hypocrisy he describes is not a Yahoo characteristic. By attributing a number of sins to "the due Course of Things," Gulliver expresses his new conviction that humanity is, as the Houyhnhnms believe, corrupt and ungovernable at heart. Humans are nothing more than beasts equipped with only enough reason to make their corruption danger-ous. But even worse than that, he says, is the inability of humanity to see its own failings, to recognize its depravity behind its false nobility.

Gulliver's apparent exemption of himself from this charge against humanity—referring to "such an Animal" rather than to humans, may be yet another moment of denial. In fact, he is guilty of the same hypocrisy he condemns, showing himself unaware of his own human flaws several times throughout his travels. He is a toady to-ward royalty in Lilliput and Brobdingnag, indifferent toward those in misery and pain when visiting the Yahoos, and ungrateful toward the kindness of strangers with the Portuguese captain, Don Pedro. Gulliver's difficulty in including himself among the humans he de-scribes as vice-ridden animals is symbolic of the identity crisis he undergoes at the end of the novel, even if he is unaware of it.

QUOTATIONS

KEY FACTS

FULL TITLE
: *Gulliver's Travels, or, Travels into Several Remote Nations of the World, by Lemuel Gulliver*

AUTHOR
: Jonathan Swift

TYPE OF WORK
: Novel

GENRE
: Satire

LANGUAGE
: English

TIME AND PLACE WRITTEN
: Approximately 1712–1726, London and Dublin

DATE OF FIRST PUBLICATION
: 1726 (1735 unabridged)

PUBLISHER
: George Faulkner (unabridged 1735 edition)

NARRATOR
: Lemuel Gulliver

POINT OF VIEW
: Gulliver speaks in the first person. He describes other characters and actions as they appear to him.

TONE
: Gulliver's tone is gullible and naïve during the first three voyages; in the fourth, it turns cynical and bitter. The intention of the author, Jonathan Swift, is satirical and biting throughout.

TENSE
: Past

SETTING (TIME)
: Early eighteenth century

SETTING (PLACE)
Primarily England and the imaginary countries of Lilliput, Blefuscu, Brobdingnag, Laputa, and the land of the Houyhnhnms

PROTAGONIST
Lemuel Gulliver

MAJOR CONFLICT
On the surface, Gulliver strives to understand the various societies with which he comes into contact and to have these societies understand his native England. Below the surface, Swift is engaged in a conflict with the English society he is satirizing.

RISING ACTION
Gulliver's encounters with other societies eventually lead up to his rejection of human society in the fourth voyage

CLIMAX
Gulliver rejects human society in the fourth voyage, specifically when he shuns the generous Don Pedro as a vulgar Yahoo

FALLING ACTION
Gulliver's unhappy return to England accentuates his alienation and compels him to buy horses, which remind him of Houyhnhnms, to keep him company

THEMES
Might versus right; the individual versus society; the limits of human understanding

MOTIFS
Excrement; foreign languages; clothing

SYMBOLS
Lilliputians; Brobdingnagians; Laputans; Houyhnhnms; England

FORESHADOWING
Gulliver's experiences with various flawed societies foreshadow his ultimate rejection of human society in the fourth voyage.

KEY FACTS

STUDY QUESTIONS

1.   *How does Swift use language and style for the purpose of satire? How does his style change as the story progresses?*

Scattered among the standard narrative style of most of Gulliver's travels are legal documents and reports, such as the inventory of Gulliver's possessions and the list of obligations presented to him by the Lilliputians. There are also brief passages in which Swift, by his style alone, ridicules the linguistic excesses of various specialists. A good example is at the beginning of Part II, Chapter I, where Gulliver uses complicated nautical jargon. The effect is so overdone that, instead of coming off as a demonstration of Gulliver's in-depth knowledge of sailing, the passage works as a satire of sailing language and, more generally, of any kind of specialist jargon. A similar passage occurs in Part III, Chapter III, where Gulliver's painstaking description of the geometry of Laputa serves as a satire of philosophical jargon.

Over the course of the novel, there are several changes in Swift's style. In the first two voyages, the style is constant: it is a relatively lighthearted but still biting satire of European culture and politics, framed as an adventure among dwarves and giants. In the third voyage, the tone shifts. Gulliver becomes less of a personality and more of an abstract observer. His judgments of the societies he encounters become more direct and unmediated, and the overall narrative becomes less of an adventure and more of a scattered satire on abstract thought. In the fourth voyage, the tone becomes, for the most part, much more serious than in the first three adventures. Gulliver too is more serious and more desperate, and his change in personality is reflected in a style that is darker, more somber, and more cynical.

2.   *Does Gulliver change as the story progresses? Does he*
     learn from his adventures?

Gulliver is somewhat more tranquil and less restless at the end of
the story than he is at the beginning. In desiring first to stay with the
Houyhnhnms, then to find an island on which he can live in exile,
Gulliver shows that his adventures have taught him that a simple
life, one without the complexities and weaknesses of human society,
may be best. At the same time, his tranquility is superficial—lying
not far below the surface is a deep distaste for humanity that is
aroused as soon as the crew of Don Pedro de Mendez captures him.
From our point of view, after we have looked at the world through
Gulliver's eyes for much of the novel, Gulliver undergoes several
interesting transformations: from the naïve Englishman to the ex-
perienced but still open-minded world traveler of the first two voyages; then to the jaded island-hopper of the third voyage; and finally
to the cynical, disillusioned, and somewhat insane misanthrope of
the fourth voyage.

3.   *Is Gulliver an everyman figure or does he have a*
     distinctive personality of his own?

In many ways, Gulliver's role as a generic human is more important than any personal opinions or abilities he may have. Fate and
circumstance conspire to lead him from place to place, while he
never really asserts his own desires. By minimizing the importance
of Gulliver as a specific person, Swift puts the focus on the social
satire itself. At the same time, Gulliver himself becomes more and
more a subject of satire as the story progresses. At the beginning,
he is a standard issue European adventurer; by the end, he has become a misanthrope who totally rejects human society. It is in the
fourth voyage that Gulliver becomes more than simply a pair of eyes
through which we see a series of unusual societies. He is, instead,
a jaded adventurer who has seen human follies—particularly that
of pride—at their most extreme, and as a result has descended into
what looks like, and probably is, a kind of madness.

How to Write
Literary Analysis

The Literary Essay: A Step-by-Step Guide

When you read for pleasure, your only goal is enjoyment. You might find yourself reading to get caught up in an exciting story, to learn about an interesting time or place, or just to pass time. Maybe you're looking for inspiration, guidance, or a reflection of your own life. There are as many different, valid ways of reading a book as there are books in the world.

When you read a work of literature in an English class, however, you're being asked to read in a special way: you're being asked to perform *literary analysis*. To analyze something means to break it down into smaller parts and then examine how those parts work, both individually and together. Literary analysis involves examining all the parts of a novel, play, short story, or poem—elements such as character, setting, tone, and imagery—and thinking about how the author uses those elements to create certain effects.

A literary essay isn't a book review: you're not being asked whether or not you liked a book or whether you'd recommend it to another reader. A literary essay also isn't like the kind of book report you wrote when you were younger, where your teacher wanted you to summarize the book's action. A high school- or college-level literary essay asks, "How does this piece of literature actually work?" "How does it do what it does?" and, "Why might the author have made the choices he or she did?"

The Seven Steps
No one is born knowing how to analyze literature; it's a skill you learn and a process you can master. As you gain more practice with this kind of thinking and writing, you'll be able to craft a method that works best for you. But until then, here are seven basic steps to writing a well-constructed literary essay:

1. *Ask questions*
2. *Collect evidence*
3. *Construct a thesis*

4. *Develop and organize arguments*
5. *Write the introduction*
6. *Write the body paragraphs*
7. *Write the conclusion*

---

1. Ask Questions

When you're assigned a literary essay in class, your teacher will often provide you with a list of writing prompts. Lucky you! Now all you have to do is choose one. Do yourself a favor and pick a topic that interests you. You'll have a much better (not to mention easier) time if you start off with something you enjoy thinking about. If you are asked to come up with a topic by yourself, though, you might start to feel a little panicked. Maybe you have too many ideas—or none at all. Don't worry. Take a deep breath and start by asking yourself these questions:

- **What struck you?** Did a particular image, line, or scene linger in your mind for a long time? If it fascinated you, chances are you can draw on it to write a fascinating essay.

- **What confused you?** Maybe you were surprised to see a character act in a certain way, or maybe you didn't understand why the book ended the way it did. Confusing moments in a work of literature are like a loose thread in a sweater: if you pull on it, you can unravel the entire thing. Ask yourself why the author chose to write about that character or scene the way he or she did and you might tap into some important insights about the work as a whole.

- **Did you notice any patterns?** Is there a phrase that the main character uses constantly or an image that repeats throughout the book? If you can figure out how that pattern weaves through the work and what the significance of that pattern is, you've almost got your entire essay mapped out.

- **Did you notice any contradictions or ironies?** Great works of literature are complex; great literary essays recognize and explain those complexities. Maybe the title (*Happy Days*) totally disagrees with the book's subject matter (hungry orphans dying in the woods). Maybe the main character acts one way around his family and a completely different way around his friends and associates. If you can find a way to explain a work's contradictory elements, you've got the seeds of a great essay.

At this point, you don't need to know exactly what you're going to say about your topic; you just need a place to begin your exploration. You can help direct your reading and brainstorming by formulating your topic as a *question,* which you'll then try to answer in your essay. The best questions invite critical debates and discussions, not just a rehashing of the summary. Remember, you're looking for something you can *prove or argue* based on evidence you find in the text. Finally, remember to keep the scope of your question in mind: is this a topic you can adequately address within the word or page limit you've been given? Conversely, is this a topic big enough to fill the required length?

GOOD QUESTIONS

> *"Are Romeo and Juliet's parents responsible for the deaths of their children?"*
>
> *"Why do pigs keep showing up in* LORD OF THE FLIES*?"*
>
> *"Are Dr. Frankenstein and his monster alike? How?"*

BAD QUESTIONS

> *"What happens to Scout in* TO KILL A MOCKINGBIRD*?"*
>
> *"What do the other characters in* JULIUS CAESAR *think about Caesar?"*
>
> *"How does Hester Prynne in* THE SCARLET LETTER *remind me of my sister?"*

---

2. COLLECT EVIDENCE

Once you know what question you want to answer, it's time to scour the book for things that will help you answer the question. Don't worry if you don't know what you want to say yet—right now you're just collecting ideas and material and letting it all percolate. Keep track of passages, symbols, images, or scenes that deal with your topic. Eventually, you'll start making connections between these examples and your thesis will emerge.

Here's a brief summary of the various parts that compose each and every work of literature. These are the elements that you will analyze in your essay, and which you will offer as evidence to support your arguments. For more on the parts of literary works, see the Glossary of Literary Terms at the end of this section.

LITERARY ANALYSIS

ELEMENTS OF STORY   These are the *what*s of the work—what happens, where it happens, and to whom it happens.

- **Plot:** All of the events and actions of the work.

- **Character:** The people who act and are acted upon in a literary work. The main character of a work is known as the *protagonist.*

- **Conflict:** The central tension in the work. In most cases, the protagonist wants something, while opposing forces (antagonists) hinder the protagonist's progress.

- **Setting:** When and where the work takes place. Elements of setting include location, time period, time of day, weather, social atmosphere, and economic conditions.

- **Narrator:** The person telling the story. The narrator may straightforwardly report what happens, convey the subjective opinions and perceptions of one or more characters, or provide commentary and opinion in his or her own voice.

- **Themes:** The main idea or message of the work—usually an abstract idea about people, society, or life in general. A work may have many themes, which may be in tension with one another.

ELEMENTS OF STYLE   These are the *how*s—how the characters speak, how the story is constructed, and how language is used throughout the work.

- **Structure and organization:** How the parts of the work are assembled. Some novels are narrated in a linear, chronological fashion, while others skip around in time. Some plays follow a traditional three- or five-act structure, while others are a series of loosely connected scenes. Some authors deliberately leave gaps in their works, leaving readers to puzzle out the missing information. A work's structure and organization can tell you a lot about the kind of message it wants to convey.

- **Point of view:** The perspective from which a story is told. In *first-person point of view,* the narrator involves him or herself in the story. ("I went to the store"; "We watched in horror as the bird slammed into the window.") A first-person narrator is usually the protagonist of the work, but not always. In *third-person point of view,* the narrator does not participate in the story. A third-person narrator may closely follow a specific character, recounting that individual character's thoughts or experiences, or it may be what we call an *omniscient* narrator. Omniscient narrators see and know all: they can witness any event in any time or place and are privy to the inner thoughts and feelings of all characters. Remember that the narrator and the author are not the same thing!

- **Diction:** Word choice. Whether a character uses dry, clinical language or flowery prose with lots of exclamation points can tell you a lot about his or her attitude and personality.

- **Syntax:** Word order and sentence construction. Syntax is a crucial part of establishing an author's narrative voice. Ernest Hemingway, for example, is known for writing in very short, straightforward sentences, while James Joyce characteristically wrote in long, incredibly complicated lines.

- **Tone:** The mood or feeling of the text. Diction and syntax often contribute to the tone of a work. A novel written in short, clipped sentences that use small, simple words might feel brusque, cold, or matter-of-fact.

- **Imagery:** Language that appeals to the senses, representing things that can be seen, smelled, heard, tasted, or touched.

- **Figurative language:** Language that is not meant to be interpreted literally. The most common types of figurative language are *metaphors* and *similes,* which compare two unlike things in order to suggest a similarity between them— for example, "All the world's a stage," or "The moon is like a ball of green cheese." (Metaphors say one thing *is* another thing; similes claim that one thing is *like* another thing.)

---

3. CONSTRUCT A THESIS

When you've examined all the evidence you've collected and know how you want to answer the question, it's time to write your thesis statement. A *thesis* is a claim about a work of literature that needs to be supported by evidence and arguments. The thesis statement is the heart of the literary essay, and the bulk of your paper will be spent trying to prove this claim. A good thesis will be:

- **Arguable.** "*The Great Gatsby* describes New York society in the 1920s" isn't a thesis—it's a fact.

- **Provable through textual evidence**. "*Hamlet* is a confusing but ultimately very well-written play" is a weak thesis because it offers the writer's personal opinion about the book. Yes, it's arguable, but it's not a claim that can be proved or supported with examples taken from the play itself.

- **Surprising**. "Both George and Lenny change a great deal in *Of Mice and Men*" is a weak thesis because it's obvious. A really strong thesis will argue for a reading of the text that is not immediately apparent.

- **Specific**. "Dr. Frankenstein's monster tells us a lot about the human condition" is *almost* a really great thesis statement, but it's still too vague. What does the writer mean by "a lot"? *How* does the monster tell us so much about the human condition?

GOOD THESIS STATEMENTS

Question: In *Romeo and Juliet*, which is more powerful in shaping the lovers' story: fate or foolishness?

Thesis: "Though Shakespeare defines Romeo and Juliet as 'star-crossed lovers' and images of stars and planets appear throughout the play, a closer examination of that celestial imagery reveals that the stars are merely witnesses to the characters' foolish activities and not the causes themselves."

Question: How does the bell jar function as a symbol in Sylvia Plath's *The Bell Jar*?

Thesis: "A bell jar is a bell-shaped glass that has three basic uses: to hold a specimen for observation, to contain gases, and to maintain a vacuum. The bell jar appears in each of these capacities in *The Bell Jar*, Plath's semi-autobiographical novel, and each appearance marks a different stage in Esther's mental breakdown."

Question: Would Piggy in *The Lord of the Flies* make a good island leader if he were given the chance?

Thesis: "Though the intelligent, rational, and innovative Piggy has the mental characteristics of a good leader, he ultimately lacks the social skills necessary to be an effective one. Golding emphasizes this point by giving Piggy a foil in the charismatic Jack, whose magnetic personality allows him to capture and wield power effectively, if not always wisely."

---

4. DEVELOP AND ORGANIZE ARGUMENTS

The reasons and examples that support your thesis will form the middle paragraphs of your essay. Since you can't really write your thesis statement until you know how you'll structure your argument, you'll probably end up working on steps 3 and 4 at the same time.

There's no single method of argumentation that will work in every context. One essay prompt might ask you to compare and contrast two characters, while another asks you to trace an image through a given work of literature. These questions require different kinds of answers and therefore different kinds of arguments. Below, we'll discuss three common kinds of essay prompts and some strategies for constructing a solid, well-argued case.

TYPES OF LITERARY ESSAYS

• **Compare and contrast**

> *Compare and contrast the characters of Huck and Jim in* THE ADVENTURES OF HUCKLEBERRY FINN.

Chances are you've written this kind of essay before. In an academic literary context, you'll organize your arguments the same way you would in any other class. You can either go *subject by subject* or *point by point*. In the former, you'll discuss one character first and then the second. In the latter, you'll choose several traits (attitude toward life, social status, images and metaphors associated with the character) and devote a paragraph to each. You may want to use a mix of these two approaches—for example, you may want to spend a paragraph a piece broadly sketching Huck's and Jim's personalities before transitioning into a paragraph or two that describes a few key points of comparison. This can be a highly effective strategy if you want to make a counterintuitive argument—that, despite seeming to be totally different, the two objects being compared are actually similar in a very important way (or vice versa). Remember that your essay should reveal something fresh or unexpected about the text, so think beyond the obvious parallels and differences.

• **Trace**

> *Choose an image—for example, birds, knives, or eyes—and trace that image throughout* MACBETH.

Sounds pretty easy, right? All you need to do is read the play, underline every appearance of a knife in *Macbeth*, and then list them in your essay in the order they appear, right? Well, not exactly. Your teacher doesn't want a simple catalog of examples. He or she wants to see you make *connections* between those examples—that's the difference between summarizing and analyzing. In the *Macbeth* example above, think about the different contexts in which knives appear in the play and to what effect. In *Macbeth*, there are real knives and imagined knives; knives that kill and knives that simply threaten. Categorize and classify your examples to give them some order. Finally, always keep the overall effect in mind. After you choose and analyze your examples, you should come to some greater understanding about the work, as well as your chosen image, symbol, or phrase's role in developing the major themes and stylistic strategies of that work.

- **Debate**

  Is the society depicted in 1984 good for its citizens?

  In this kind of essay, you're being asked to debate a moral, ethical, or aesthetic issue regarding the work. You might be asked to judge a character or group of characters (*Is Caesar responsible for his own demise?*) or the work itself (*Is* JANE EYRE *a feminist novel?*). For this kind of essay, there are two important points to keep in mind. First, don't simply base your arguments on your personal feelings and reactions. Every literary essay expects you to read and analyze the work, so search for evidence in the text. What do characters in *1984* have to say about the government of Oceania? What images does Orwell use that might give you a hint about his attitude toward the government? As in any debate, you also need to make sure that you define all the necessary terms before you begin to argue your case. What does it mean to be a "good" society? What makes a novel "feminist"? You should define your terms right up front, in the first paragraph after your introduction.

  Second, remember that strong literary essays make contrary and surprising arguments. Try to think outside the box. In the *1984* example above, it seems like the obvious answer would be no, the totalitarian society depicted in Orwell's novel is *not* good for its citizens. But can you think of any arguments for the opposite side? Even if your final assertion is that the novel depicts a cruel, repressive, and therefore harmful society, acknowledging and responding to the counterargument will strengthen your overall case.

---

5. WRITE THE INTRODUCTION

Your introduction sets up the entire essay. It's where you present your topic and articulate the particular issues and questions you'll be addressing. It's also where you, as the writer, introduce yourself to your readers. A persuasive literary essay immediately establishes its writer as a knowledgeable, authoritative figure.

An introduction can vary in length depending on the overall length of the essay, but in a traditional five-paragraph essay it should be no longer than one paragraph. However long it is, your introduction needs to:

- **Provide any necessary context.** Your introduction should situate the reader and let him or her know what to expect. What book are you discussing? Which characters? What topic will you be addressing?

- **Answer the "So what?" question.** Why is this topic important, and why is your particular position on the topic noteworthy? Ideally, your introduction should pique the reader's interest by suggesting how your argument is surprising or otherwise counterintuitive. Literary essays make unexpected connections and reveal less-than-obvious truths.

- **Present your thesis.** This usually happens at or very near the end of your introduction.

- **Indicate the shape of the essay to come.** Your reader should finish reading your introduction with a good sense of the scope of your essay as well as the path you'll take toward proving your thesis. You don't need to spell out every step, but you do need to suggest the organizational pattern you'll be using.

Your introduction should not:

- **Be vague.** Beware of the two killer words in literary analysis: *interesting* and *important*. Of course the work, question, or example is interesting and important—that's why you're writing about it!

- **Open with any grandiose assertions.** Many student readers think that beginning their essays with a flamboyant statement such as, "Since the dawn of time, writers have been fascinated with the topic of free will," makes them sound important and commanding. You know what? It actually sounds pretty amateurish.

- **Wildly praise the work.** Another typical mistake student writers make is extolling the work or author. Your teacher doesn't need to be told that "Shakespeare is perhaps the greatest writer in the English language." You can mention a work's reputation in passing—by referring to *The Adventures of Huckleberry Finn* as "Mark Twain's enduring classic," for example—but don't make a point of bringing it up unless that reputation is key to your argument.

- **Go off-topic.** Keep your introduction streamlined and to the point. Don't feel the need to throw in all kinds of bells and whistles in order to impress your reader—just get to the point as quickly as you can, without skimping on any of the required steps.

---

6. Write the Body Paragraphs

Once you've written your introduction, you'll take the arguments you developed in step 4 and turn them into your body paragraphs. The organization of this middle section of your essay will largely be determined by the argumentative strategy you use, but no matter how you arrange your thoughts, your body paragraphs need to do the following:

- **Begin with a strong topic sentence.** Topic sentences are like signs on a highway: they tell the reader where they are and where they're going. A good topic sentence not only alerts readers to what issue will be discussed in the following paragraph but also gives them a sense of what argument will be made *about* that issue. "Rumor and gossip play an important role in *The Crucible*" isn't a strong topic sentence because it doesn't tell us very much. "The community's constant gossiping creates an environment that allows false accusations to flourish" is a much stronger topic sentence— it not only tells us *what* the paragraph will discuss (gossip) but *how* the paragraph will discuss the topic (by showing how gossip creates a set of conditions that leads to the play's climactic action).

- **Fully and completely develop a single thought.** Don't skip around in your paragraph or try to stuff in too much material. Body paragraphs are like bricks: each individual one needs to be strong and sturdy or the entire structure will collapse. Make sure you have really proven your point before moving on to the next one.

- **Use transitions effectively.** Good literary essay writers know that each paragraph must be clearly and strongly linked to the material around it. Think of each paragraph as a response to the one that precedes it. Use transition words and phrases such as *however, similarly, on the contrary, therefore,* and *furthermore* to indicate what kind of response you're making.

---

7. WRITE THE CONCLUSION

Just as you used the introduction to ground your readers in the topic before providing your thesis, you'll use the conclusion to quickly summarize the specifics learned thus far and then hint at the broader implications of your topic. A good conclusion will:

- **Do more than simply restate the thesis.** If your thesis argued that *The Catcher in the Rye* can be read as a Christian allegory, don't simply end your essay by saying, "And that is why *The Catcher in the Rye* can be read as a Christian allegory." If you've constructed your arguments well, this kind of statement will just be redundant.

- **Synthesize the arguments, not summarize them.** Similarly, don't repeat the details of your body paragraphs in your conclusion. The reader has already read your essay, and chances are it's not so long that they've forgotten all your points by now.

- **Revisit the "So what?" question.** In your introduction, you made a case for why your topic and position are important. You should close your essay with the same sort of gesture. What do your readers know now that they didn't know before? How will that knowledge help them better appreciate or understand the work overall?

- **Move from the specific to the general.** Your essay has most likely treated a very specific element of the work—a single character, a small set of images, or a particular passage. In your conclusion, try to show how this narrow discussion has wider implications for the work overall. If your essay on *To Kill a Mockingbird* focused on the character of Boo Radley, for example, you might want to include a bit in your conclusion about how he fits into the novel's larger message about childhood, innocence, or family life.

- **Stay relevant.** Your conclusion should suggest new directions of thought, but it shouldn't be treated as an opportunity to pad your essay with all the extra, interesting ideas you came up with during your brainstorming sessions but couldn't fit into the essay proper. Don't attempt to stuff in unrelated queries or too many abstract thoughts.

- **Avoid making overblown closing statements.** A conclusion should open up your highly specific, focused discussion, but it should do so without drawing a sweeping lesson about life or human nature. Making such observations may be part of the point of reading, but it's almost always a mistake in essays, where these observations tend to sound overly dramatic or simply silly.

A+ ESSAY CHECKLIST

Congratulations! If you've followed all the steps we've outlined above, you should have a solid literary essay to show for all your efforts. What if you've got your sights set on an A+? To write the kind of superlative essay that will be rewarded with a perfect grade, keep the following rubric in mind. These are the qualities that teachers expect to see in a truly A+ essay. How does yours stack up?

- ✓ Demonstrates a thorough understanding of the book
- ✓ Presents an original, compelling argument
- ✓ Thoughtfully analyzes the text's formal elements
- ✓ Uses appropriate and insightful examples
- ✓ Structures ideas in a logical and progressive order
- ✓ Demonstrates a mastery of sentence construction, transitions, grammar, spelling, and word choice

LITERARY ANALYSIS

SUGGESTED ESSAY TOPICS

1.   Why is Gulliver so eager to assert his own country's importance to the Brobdingnagians? How does this desire compare to the Lilliputians' desire to assert their importance to Gulliver?

2.   What is the significance, if any, of the order in which Gulliver's journeys take place? How does each adventure build on the previous one?

3.   What is the allegorical significance of the floating island of Laputa?

4.   Why does Gulliver keep traveling despite his many misfortunes?

5.   Why does Gulliver want to stay with the Houyhnhnms? Does his desire make sense in light of the other societies he has visited?

6.   How do the Lilliputians view the threat that Gulliver represents?

A+ Student Essay

> Who are the Slamecksans, and who are the citizens of
> Blefuscu? In what ways are these characters similar? How
> does the pairing of these characters illuminate the satire's
> major themes?

The comedy of Jonathan Swift's Slamecksans derives from the tension between their silly problems and the grave language in which
these problems are described. Likewise, the Blefuscu episode is humorous because it marries a serious reporter's voice with an incredibly trivial subject. Much of Swift's comedy follows the pattern of
the Slamecksan and Blefuscu episodes, poking fun at minor sources
of major human anxieties. The Slamecksans and the citizens of Blefuscu thus concisely demonstrate Swift's comic method as well as
his interest in the common human tendency to overreact to mildly
stressful situations.

Although the concerns of the Lilliputian political faction known
as the Slamecksans are negligible, Swift uses them as a source of high
comedy by describing them in an incongruously grave manner.
The tiny man who approaches Lemuel Gulliver to tell him about
the Slamecksans wears a look of distress, but Swift undercuts the
messenger's concerns by pointing out that Lemuel must first offer to
position his ear close to the tiny sentinel, then pick up the sentinel
and hold him close to his face. The small man's speech contains
serious political language, including references to factions and the
national Constitution, but Swift undercuts the momentousness
of the speech by pointing out that the issue at hand is a conflict
between wearers of high and low heels. The messenger makes a
worrisome reference to mixed signals from a powerful political figure, but Swift makes these signals ridiculous when he forces us to
visualize a man wobbling on a mismatched pair of high- and low-
heeled shoes. By pairing recognizably dry, political jargon with the
absurd subject of shoe preferences, Swift encourages his readers to
laugh at the seriousness with which people regard factional disputes
in the real world.

Similarly, the description of the Lilliputians' war with Blefuscu
involves a hilarious mixing of sober diction and a ludicrous topic.
Swift somberly notes that 30,000 little people have died in the war
with Blefuscu, but he undermines the impact of the statistic when

he points out that the people were fighting over the proper way to crack an egg. Swift triggers readers' thoughts of crucial Constitutional debates when he alludes to the disagreement between Lilliput and Blefescu over the interpretation of the Blefescu's doctrine, the *Brundrecral,* but he again subverts expectations of high drama by hilariously noting that the phrase in question is: "All true believers shall crack their eggs at the convenient end." Swift gravely refers to the origins of the tension with Blefuscu, but he again makes the matter ridiculous when he points out that decades of strife resulted from one Lilliputian having cut his finger on an eggshell. Again, Swift finds comedy in the juxtaposition of formal language and trivial subjects, and in doing so, implicitly encourages readers to laugh at the petty struggles and obsessions that characterize political life in the real world.

Throughout Lemuel's travels in Lilliput, Swift employs this jarring combination of subject and tone to poke fun at self-dramatizing behavior. The Lilliputians take great pride in their military parade, but Swift exposes the foolishness of their grandiose actions by dryly pointing out that they must walk through the legs of Lemuel's tattered pants (and thus underneath his genitals) as they march. The peevish demands of Skyresh are related in the most objective, solemn language, but Swift makes his concerns ridiculous by reminding us that he has no real control over Lemuel, his gigantic "prisoner." The Lilliputians revere and honor their towering emperor, but Swift encourages us to laugh at the monarch by noting that he is merely fractions of an inch taller than the other citizens and that he dresses in garish, preposterous clothing.

Through these ludicrous episodes, Swift leads readers to do more than laugh—he encourages them to apply their laughter to the real world and to reflect on the gravity with which full-size people often regard their own, ultimately Lilliputian lives. The European landscape of Swift's day was being ravaged by political, religious, and ethnic tensions. While none of these issues are as frivolous a case for war as egg-cracking etiquette or heel height, Swift's satire urges readers to examine their grievances carefully before acting upon them—lest they become as laughable as the Lilliputians.

LITERARY ANALYSIS

GLOSSARY OF LITERARY TERMS

ANTAGONIST
> The entity that acts to frustrate the goals of the *protagonist*. The antagonist is usually another *character* but may also be a non-human force.

ANTIHERO / ANTIHEROINE
> A *protagonist* who is not admirable or who challenges notions of what should be considered admirable.

CHARACTER
> A person, animal, or any other thing with a personality that appears in a *narrative*.

CLIMAX
> The moment of greatest intensity in a text or the major turning point in the *plot*.

CONFLICT
> The central struggle that moves the *plot* forward. The conflict can be the *protagonist*'s struggle against fate, nature, society, or another person.

FIRST-PERSON POINT OF VIEW
> A literary style in which the *narrator* tells the story from his or her own *point of view* and refers to himself or herself as "I." The narrator may be an active participant in the story or just an observer.

HERO / HEROINE
> The principal *character* in a literary work or *narrative*.

IMAGERY
> Language that brings to mind sense-impressions, representing things that can be seen, smelled, heard, tasted, or touched.

MOTIF
> A recurring idea, structure, contrast, or device that develops or informs the major *themes* of a work of literature.

NARRATIVE
> A story.

NARRATOR

The person (sometimes a *character*) who tells a story; the *voice* assumed by the writer. The narrator and the author of the work of literature are not the same person.

PLOT

The arrangement of the events in a story, including the sequence in which they are told, the relative emphasis they are given, and the causal connections between events.

POINT OF VIEW

The *perspective* that a *narrative* takes toward the events it describes.

PROTAGONIST

The main *character* around whom the story revolves.

SETTING

The location of a *narrative* in time and space. Setting creates mood or atmosphere.

SUBPLOT

A secondary *plot* that is of less importance to the overall story but may serve as a point of contrast or comparison to the main plot.

SYMBOL

An object, *character,* figure, or color that is used to represent an abstract idea or concept. Unlike an *emblem,* a symbol may have different meanings in different contexts.

SYNTAX

The way the words in a piece of writing are put together to form lines, phrases, or clauses; the basic structure of a piece of writing.

THEME

A fundamental and universal idea explored in a literary work.

TONE

The author's attitude toward the subject or *characters* of a story or poem or toward the reader.

VOICE

An author's individual way of using language to reflect his or her own personality and attitudes. An author communicates voice through *tone, diction,* and *syntax.*

A Note on Plagiarism

Plagiarism—presenting someone else's work as your own—rears its ugly head in many forms. Many students know that copying text without citing it is unacceptable. But some don't realize that even if you're not quoting directly, but instead are paraphrasing or summarizing, *it is plagiarism* unless you cite the source.

Here are the most common forms of plagiarism:

- Using an author's phrases, sentences, or paragraphs without citing the source
- Paraphrasing an author's ideas without citing the source
- Passing off another student's work as your own

How do you steer clear of plagiarism? You should *always* acknowledge all words and ideas that aren't your own by using quotation marks around verbatim text or citations like footnotes and endnotes to note another writer's ideas. For more information on how to give credit when credit is due, ask your teacher for guidance or visit www.sparknotes.com.

REVIEW & RESOURCES

QUIZ

1. How does Gulliver end up stranded in Lilliput?

   A. He survives a shipwreck
   B. His crew abandons him
   C. He is dropped there by an enormous eagle
   D. He stops there for provisions and is trapped while he sleeps

2. How do the Lilliputians offer Gulliver something to drink?

   A. They break down their town reservoir
   B. They divert a river
   C. They summon the rains
   D. They roll out barrels of wine

3. How does Gulliver earn the title of Nardac in Lilliput?

   A. By capturing the Blefuscudian fleet
   B. By putting out the fire in the empress's quarters
   C. By showing lenience toward a group of soldiers who earlier attack him
   D. By helping the Lilliputians construct a new palace

4. Instead of killing him outright, the Lilliputians decide on which of the following punishments for Gulliver?

   A. Blinding him and slowly starving him to death
   B. Exiling him
   C. Cutting off his hands
   D. Poisoning him

5. What is the line of doctrine over which the Blefuscudians and Lilliputians differ?

    A.   "All true believers shall break their eggs at the small end."

    B.   "All true believers shall break their eggs at the big end."

    C.   "All true believers shall break their eggs as they see fit."

    D.   "All true believers shall break their eggs at the convenient end."

6. Who is Gulliver's main caretaker in Brobdingnag?

    A.   The farmer

    B.   The queen

    C.   Reldresal

    D.   Glumdalclitch

7. How does Gulliver leave Brobdingnag?

    A.   He builds himself a sailboat

    B.   He is exiled

    C.   He is carried away by a giant eagle

    D.   He is taken back to England by Don Pedro

8. Who first discovers Gulliver in Brobdingnag?

    A.   The farmer

    B.   A field worker

    C.   Glumdalclitch

    D.   Lord Munodi

9. What does the farmer make Gulliver do in order to earn money?

    A.   Perform tricks for spectators

    B.   Spy on neighboring farmers

    C.   Work in the fields

    D.   Kill rats

10. Who is Gulliver's main enemy in the royal court of Brobdingnag?

    A.   The dwarf
    B.   The king
    C.   The queen
    D.   Reldresal

11. What human invention does Gulliver propose to the king of Brobdingnag that the king finds revolting?

    A.   Gunpowder
    B.   Christianity
    C.   Lawyers
    D.   Lying

12. How does Gulliver end up in Laputa?

    A.   Pirates attack his ship
    B.   His crew mutinies
    C.   He is shipwrecked
    D.   He stops there for provisions

13. What do "flappers" do for the people of Laputa?

    A.   Keep them cool by fanning them
    B.   Protect them from birds and insects
    C.   Keep them engaged in conversations
    D.   Introduce them to other people

14. Why does Gulliver seem stupid to the Laputans?

    A.   He does not speak their language
    B.   He is ignorant of music and mathematics
    C.   He is unwilling to use a flapper
    D.   He does not understand how the floating island works

15. Why does Gulliver summon the shades of René Descartes and Pierre Gassendi to talk to Aristotle?

    A. Descartes and Gassendi were supporters of Aristotle's theories
    B. Descartes, Gassendi, and Aristotle were all political satirists
    C. Descartes and Gassendi were philosophers who revised many of Aristotle's theories
    D. Descartes and Gassendi were friends of Swift

16. Why is Gulliver exiled from the land of the Houyhnhnms?

    A. He urinates on the queen's palace
    B. He steals from his Houyhnhnm master
    C. The Houyhnhnms decide that it is not right for a Yahoo to live among them
    D. The Houyhnhnms decide to exterminate the Yahoos

17. Why is Lord Munodi looked down upon by the government in Lagado?

    A. He uses traditional methods of agriculture and architecture
    B. He is ignorant of music and mathematics
    C. He breaks his eggs on the little end
    D. He once tried to lead a coup against the current government

18. Who are Gulliver's closest friends after he returns from his time with the Houyhnhnms?

    A. His wife and children
    B. Lord Munodi
    C. Two horses
    D. Don Pedro de Mendez

19. How does the king of Luggnagg dispose of his enemies in the court?

    A.   By slipping poison into the wine they drink to his health

    B.   By poisoning the floor they are required to lick as they approach him

    C.   By poisoning their clothes

    D.   By exiling them from the island

20. On which island is Gulliver given the opportunity to summon the shades of the dead?

    A.   Luggnagg

    B.   Glubbdubdrib

    C.   Laputa

    D.   Lagado

21. What is different about the Struldbrugs of Luggnagg?

    A.   They are immortal

    B.   They are blind

    C.   They have no capacity for memory

    D.   They have no need to consume food

22. Which of the following kinds of specialized language does Swift not ridicule?

    A.   Legal

    B.   Naval

    C.   Culinary

    D.   Scientific

23. Which of the human societies that he visits does Gulliver find most appealing?

    A.   Lagado

    B.   Brobdingnag

    C.   England

    D.   Blefuscu

24. Which of the following adjectives best describe Gulliver's personality in the first three voyages?

    A. Direct and perspicacious
    B. Cynical and bitter
    C. Gullible and honest
    D. Kind and condescending

25. Which of the following places does Gulliver visit last?

    A. Brobdingnag
    B. Lilliput
    C. Houyhnhnmland
    D. Laputa

Suggestions for Further Reading

FOX, CHRISTOPHER. *The Cambridge Companion to Jonathan Swift*. Cambridge: Cambridge University Press, 2003.

HAMMOND, BREAN S. *Gulliver's Travels*. Philadelphia: Open University Press, 1988.

HINNANT, CHARLES H. *Purity and Defilement in* GULLIVER'S TRAVELS. London: Macmillan, 1987.

KNOWLES, RONALD. GULLIVER'S TRAVELS: *The Politics of Satire*. New York: Twayne Publishers, 1996.

LOCK, F. P. *The Politics of* GULLIVER'S TRAVELS. Oxford: Clarendon Press, 1980.

LUND, ROGER. *Jonathan Swift's* GULLIVER'S TRAVELS: *A Sourcebook*. New York: Routledge, 2006.

RAWSON, CLAUDE JULIEN. *God, Gulliver, and Genocide: Barbarism and the European Imagination*. New York and Oxford: Oxford University Press, 2001.

SMITH, FREDERICK N., ed. *The Genres of* GULLIVER'S TRAVELS. Newark, Delaware: University of Delaware Press, 1990.

TIPPETT, BRIAN. *Gulliver's Travels*. Basingstoke, England: Macmillan, 1989.

REVIEW & RESOURCES